Perspectives on Teaching and Learning Leadership in Higher Education

Perspectives on Teaching and Learning Leadership in Higher Education has been designed to bring together case studies to facilitate the development of effective and well-equipped leaders within the higher education sector.

With the growing global emphasis on higher education to improve the quality of the learning experience for increasingly diverse students, this book focuses on good leadership in teaching and learning by illustrating the lived experiences of academics and sharing case studies which highlight moments and instances that positively impacted their professional development as leaders. The globally relevant case studies included provide insights into the different ideas implemented by leaders for learning and teaching projects. Through these case studies, the decision-making processes of leaders are made visible to other aspiring leaders in similar positions.

This resource will be invaluable in enhancing and enriching the learning experience of students, as this book demonstrates that academic leadership is intricately related to student learning. It will help leaders negotiate their own conflicts and challenges and will be essential reading for present and budding learning and teaching leaders in the educational sector.

Josephine Lang is Associate Professor and Academic Director of Educational Innovation in the Melbourne School of Professional and Continuing Education at the University of Melbourne, Australia.

Namrata Rao is Principal Lecturer in Education and Coordinator of the Postgraduate Taught Programmes within the School of Education at Liverpool Hope University, UK.

Anesa Hosein is Associate Professor in Higher Education and the Head of Educational Development and Research, University of Surrey, UK.

The Staff and Educational Development Association Focus Series

Series Editor: Stephen Powell

The SEDA Focus series is for everyone interested in teaching, learning and assessment in higher education. Books in the Series are scholarly and practical, written by educational developers and researchers on up-to-the minute topics, bringing together experience and practice in a theoretical context. The Series is for educational, academic, staff and faculty developers, subject academics developing their professional teaching interests, institutional managers and everyone working to improve the quality of student learning. SEDA (The Staff and Educational Development Association) is the long-established professional association for staff and educational developers in the UK, promoting innovation and good practice in higher education.

Titles in the series:

Perspectives on Teaching and Learning Leadership in Higher Education
Case Studies from UK and Australia
Edited by Josephine Lang, Namrata Rao and Anesa Hosein

Active Learning in Higher Education
Theoretical Considerations and Perspectives
Edited by Wendy Garnham and Isobel Gowers

For more information about this series, please visit: www.routledge.com/SEDA-Focus/book-series/SEDAF

Perspectives on Teaching and Learning Leadership in Higher Education
Case Studies from UK and Australia

Edited by Josephine Lang,
Namrata Rao and Anesa Hosein

LONDON AND NEW YORK

First published 2024
by Routledge
4 Park Square, Milton Park, Abingdon, Oxon OX14 4RN

and by Routledge
605 Third Avenue, New York, NY 10158

Routledge is an imprint of the Taylor & Francis Group, an informa business

© 2024 selection and editorial matter, Josephine Lang, Namrata Rao and Anesa Hosein; individual chapters, the contributors

The right of Josephine Lang, Namrata Rao and Anesa Hosein to be identified as the authors of the editorial material, and of the authors for their individual chapters, has been asserted in accordance with sections 77 and 78 of the Copyright, Designs and Patents Act 1988.

All rights reserved. No part of this book may be reprinted or reproduced or utilised in any form or by any electronic, mechanical, or other means, now known or hereafter invented, including photocopying and recording, or in any information storage or retrieval system, without permission in writing from the publishers.

Trademark notice: Product or corporate names may be trademarks or registered trademarks, and are used only for identification and explanation without intent to infringe.

British Library Cataloguing-in-Publication Data
A catalogue record for this book is available from the British Library

Library of Congress Cataloging-in-Publication Data
Names: Lang, Josephine, 1965– editor. | Rao, Namrata (Lecturer in education), editor. | Hosein, Anesa, editor.
Title: Perspectives on teaching and learning leadership in higher education: case studies from UK and Australia / edited by Josephine Lang, Namrata Rao, and Anesa Hosein.
Description: Abingdon, Oxon; New York, NY: Routledge, 2024. | Series: The Staff and Educational Development Association focus series | Includes bibliographical references and index.
Identifiers: LCCN 2023017573 (print) | LCCN 2023017574 (ebook) | ISBN 9781032418421 (hardback) | ISBN 9781032418438 (paperback) | ISBN 9781003360018 (ebook)
Subjects: LCSH: Universities and colleges—Great Britain—Administration—Case studies. | Universities and colleges—Australia—Administration—Case studies. | College teaching—Great Britain—Case studies. | College teaching—Australia—Case studies. | Educational leadership—Great Britain—Case studies. | Educational leadership—Australia—Case studies.
Classification: LCC LB2341.8.G7 P47 2024 (print) | LCC LB2341.8.G7 (ebook) | DDC 378.1/010941—dc23/eng/20230512
LC record available at https://lccn.loc.gov/2023017573
LC ebook record available at https://lccn.loc.gov/2023017574

ISBN: 978-1-032-41842-1 (hbk)
ISBN: 978-1-032-41843-8 (pbk)
ISBN: 978-1-003-36001-8 (ebk)

DOI: 10.4324/9781003360018

Typeset in Times New Roman
by Apex CoVantage, LLC

Contents

List of tables	vii
Notes on the contributors	viii
Foreword	xi
ELIZABETH JOHNSON	
Acknowledgements	xiii

PART I
Introduction   1

1 Teaching and learning leadership in higher education: an introduction   3
JOSEPHINE LANG AND ANESA HOSEIN

PART II
Case studies on teaching and learning leadership   13

2 Pragmatic leadership for collaboration in a competitive sector: the case of sigma   15
DUNCAN LAWSON

3 Leading for inclusivity: peer-assisted learning and internationalisation   24
GITA SEDGHI

4 Stepping stones towards higher education teaching and learning leadership: a case study on becoming a Deputy Dean   33
LUCIA ZUNDANS-FRASER

5 Opportunities and barriers to leadership in student
  support services: a case study of inclusive assessment   41
  SILVIA COLAIACOMO AND TOM SHARP

6 Be(com)ing an academic leader: a case study on a
  collaborative partnership for external peer review   49
  JOSEPHINE LANG

7 Leading as an international academic: a case study of a
  casual teaching team   58
  JASVIR KAUR NACHATAR SINGH

8 A leadership quest in teaching and learning: a case
  study of building capability and competency   66
  BARBARA C. PANTHER

PART III
Implications for practice   75

9 Conclusion: perspectives on teaching and learning
  leadership in higher education: implications for practice   77
  JOSEPHINE LANG AND NAMRATA RAO

  Index   *84*

Tables

1.1 Leadership case studies 8
6.1 Analysis of academic leadership categories (Juntrasook, 2014) in my lived experience of be(com)ing an academic leader in higher education through NADLATE example 55
9.1 Competing paradigms informing teaching and learning leadership (adapted from Harris & Cullen, 2010, Chapters 2 and 3) 79

Contributors

Silvia Colaiacomo is a lecturer and programme director in the Arena Centre for Research-Based Education at University College London, UCL. Her background is in history of art and modern foreign languages, which she taught in higher education in the UK and internationally. Since 2016, she has been focusing on academic development programmes for teaching and support staff. She is particularly interested in internationalisation of the curriculum, intercultural communicative skills and exploring the interaction between space, pedagogy and technology in different disciplinary settings.

Anesa Hosein is Associate Professor and the Head of Educational Development and Research at the University of Surrey's Institute of Education. In her role, she leads a programme of activities that helps develop teaching staff's pedagogical knowledge, practice and research across the university. Anesa researches how marginalised identities affect higher education participation for both students and academics. Her current research is around investigating migrant academics as well as student mental health.

Josephine Lang is Associate Professor and Academic Director of Educational Innovation in Melbourne School of Professional and Continuing Education at the University of Melbourne, Australia. In this role, she leads and works with the university's faculties to facilitate the development of their Continuing Professional Education portfolio of courses. Her research expertise is in the areas of professional learning, curriculum, pedagogy and assessment. She is now focusing on bringing all this expertise to bear to lead, research and apply to the emerging field of digital micro-credentials; this includes engaging key stakeholders within the micro-credential and skills ecosystems to deliver quality digital micro-credentials for lifelong learning. Josephine has held numerous academic leadership roles in teaching and learning at subject and programme levels in the sectors of university and schools. She has led collaborative partnerships of teaching- and learning-related initiatives across multiple Australian universities.

Contributors ix

Duncan Lawson is a professor at Coventry University and has over 35 years of experience in higher education. Since the early 1990s, he has been involved in the development and delivery of mathematics and statistics support, within Coventry University, across the UK, and internationally. Working closely with Professor Tony Croft (Loughborough University), he helped establish the *sigma* network, a voluntary association of mathematics and statistics support practitioners, which shares resources and provides personal development opportunities. In 2016, Professors Croft and Lawson were jointly awarded the Institute of Mathematics and Its Applications Gold Medal for their work in the development of mathematics and statistics support in higher education. In 2019, Duncan Lawson was awarded an MBE for services to mathematics in higher education.

Jasvir Kaur Nachatar Singh is an award-winning senior lecturer in the Department of Management and Marketing, La Trobe Business School, La Trobe University, Australia. In 2020, Dr Singh received international teaching recognition from Advance HE, UK, as a Fellow (FHEA). In 2018, Dr Singh received two La Trobe University Teaching Awards and the Best Presenter Award at the Global Higher Education Forum, Malaysia. Dr Singh's research expertise is in higher education, with a particular interest in exploring international students' lived experiences of academic success, employability, career aspirations and learning experiences. Dr Singh also explores the lived experiences of skilled migrants, especially international academics. Dr Singh has published numerous articles in high-impact journals and has presented at various national and international higher education conferences. In 2021, Dr Singh was appointed as a research fellow at the Malaysian National Higher Education Research Institute.

Barbie Panther is Associate Professor and Director, Teaching Capability at Deakin University, where she has responsibility for professional development, recognition and reward programmes in learning and teaching, including the Deakin Academy of Learning and Teaching. Barbie's academic background is in chemistry, and she has held leadership roles in a number of Australian universities, including Associate Dean, Learning and Teaching, for the Faculty of Science and Technology at Federation University, Australia. Barbie holds roles in teaching and learning leadership with Advance HE and the executive of the Council of Australasian Leaders of Learning and Teaching. Barbie is passionate about exploring the possibilities of digital learning, supporting the development of inclusive learning environments, and building capability and recognition programmes for those who design, deliver, enable and lead learning and teaching.

Namrata Rao is Principal Lecturer in Education at Liverpool Hope University, where she coordinates the School of Education's postgraduate taught programmes. Her key areas of research and publication include (but are not restricted to) various aspects of learning and teaching in higher education that influence academic identity and academic practice. She is a senior fellow of the Higher Education Academy, co-convener of the Learning, Teaching and Assessment Network of the Society for Research in Higher Education and member of the Research and Development group of the Association for Learning Development in Higher Education. Her recent publications include a co-edited book, *Early Career Teachers in Higher Education: International Teaching Journeys* (2021), published by Bloomsbury.

Gita Sedghi is Professor of Chemistry Education at the University of Liverpool. As the School of Physical Sciences Equality, Diversity and Inclusion Lead, she is passionate about the potential of education to promote equality, regardless of gender, ethnicity or any other protected characteristics. Her recent leadership roles are acting as the Chief Institutional Moderator for the Liverpool partner university in China and the Chair of 'Culture and Student Experience', a subgroup of the Self-Assessment Team formed to lead and oversee the work towards the university's application for an award under the Race Equality Charter. Gita's involvement in pedagogical research and learning and teaching innovations both within her discipline and more widely has been recognised by her Principal Fellowship and National Teaching Fellowship of Advance HE. Gita's research is focused on peer-assisted learning, inclusive teaching and learning, and online assessment and formative feedback to enhance students' performance and experience.

Tom Sharp is a disability practitioner with 24 years of experience in further and higher education. Starting as a support worker, his career has been spent in the development and leadership of support teams, encouraging staff and students to adopt a critical view of academic engagement in order to facilitate independent learning. Disabled students may benefit from advocacy and the opportunity to test new ways of working, and the role of the disability practitioner is to facilitate and guide the student towards autonomy within an environment that often seems foreign and inaccessible. His current role at King's College London involves the screening, referral and development of support networks for neurodivergent students.

Foreword

Over the last two decades, global participation in tertiary education has more than doubled (UNESCO, 2022). In many countries, higher education has moved from elite to mass education, with consequential expansion in the provision of learning and teaching. At the same time, universities and other higher education providers are re-imagining what their students need as the world around them changes. Global challenges in climate change, sustainability and social change intersect with the rise of digital work, life and study to require new degrees and qualifications that are relevant for contemporary learners. The accelerating pace of change places new demands on educational communities, institutions and leaders. Higher education is both a knowledge industry and a social good which requires deft leadership to maintain and grow its value to individual learners, communities and broader society.

Effective teaching and learning in higher education is intrinsically complex. It combines comprehensive and cutting-edge knowledge of subject areas with deep knowledge of how learners learn – both within a specific subject area and more generally as adult learners. Contemporary learning in higher education rests on decades of research which combines approaches from psychology, education and social sciences and is creatively captured by Bruce Macfarlane's higher education research archipelago (Macfarlane, 2022). Leading teaching and learning is equally complex as it must create and sustain a context that drives learning, engages and supports diverse learners and teachers, and is also responsive to local, regional and global influences.

Leadership in higher education shares common ground with leadership in other creative contexts, but it does have unique demands. Higher education institutions typically combine missions in learning and teaching with research or scholarship and/or professional leadership, creating another dimension in leadership development. Leadership in learning and teaching requires a specific skill set as described by Quinlan (2014), who notes three aspects of leadership needed to promote student learning: organisational development, transformative leadership and knowledge of teaching and learning. Organisational leadership skills and people leadership are common to many leadership contexts, but deep knowledge of learning and teaching and the complex environment of higher education distinguish its leadership challenges.

By its nature, higher education fosters independent and critical thought, creating fertile ground for diverse leadership approaches. Leadership comes from formally appointed roles, subject matter experts and informal leadership, with the latter often inspired by passion for a targeted outcome or approach. More recently, students have become recognised as collaborators and leaders in higher education, notably through the 'students as partners' movement (Mercer-Mapstone et al., 2017). Collaborative leadership models have been described in a range of settings, notably drawing on ideas of communities of practice and distributed leadership (Jones & Harvey, 2017). At its best, leadership in higher education creates space for diverse leaders to work together, leveraging complementary skills.

This volume describes the diversity and complexity of leadership for learning and teaching in higher education. Through its case studies, it illustrates the many paths to effective leadership and the critical importance of deep immersion in the business of higher education. The authors are drawn from universities in the United Kingdom and Australia to reflect on leadership in academic support programmes, inclusive practice, building capability for learning and teaching, and building academic networks. Importantly, these case studies present both formal and informal leadership in a variety of institutional settings, demonstrating the link between institutional and professional culture and leadership. These stories of leadership provide practical inspiration for emerging and current leaders and contribute to the understanding of effective leadership for learning and teaching in higher education.

Professor Elizabeth Johnson
Deputy Vice-Chancellor Academic
Deakin University
January 2023

References

Jones, S., & Harvey, M. (2017). Revealing the nexus between distributed leadership and communities of practice. In J. MacDonald & A. Cater-Steel (Eds.), *Communities of practice* (pp. 313–327). Springer.

Macfarlane, B. (2022). A voyage around the ideological islands of higher education research. *Higher Education Research & Development, 41*(1), 107–115.

Mercer-Mapstone, L., Dvorakova, S. L., Matthews, K. E., Abbot, S., Cheng, B., Felten, P., & Swaim, K. (2017). A systematic literature review of students as partners in higher education. *International Journal for Students as Partners, 1*(1). https://doi.org/10.15173/ijsap.v1i1.3119

Quinlan, K. M. (2014). Leadership of teaching for student learning in higher education: What is needed? *Higher Education Research & Development, 33*(1), 32–45.

UNESCO. (2022). *Higher education figures at a glance.* http://uis.unesco.org/sites/default/files/documents/f_unesco1015_brochure_web_en.pdf

Acknowledgements

This book has been an outcome of our ongoing interest in the field of academic leadership and the particular position of teaching and learning leadership within it. As editors, we have in our own ways tried to navigate our paths towards teaching and learning leadership over our time in academia and recognise from our own lives the micro-moments that have been key to the way we have positioned ourselves as teaching and learning leaders. However, we were equally curious to hear from others about their instances of having to lead. This curiosity led to our initial proposal to Staff Education Development Organisation (SEDA) to consider a publication of case studies in leadership for the Society. However, it was SEDA that identified this as a worthy proposal to be considered for publication as a book with Routledge. We are grateful to SEDA and in particular to Stephen Powell and James Wisdom for their support in helping us to develop this proposal into a book. We also owe a particular thanks to the Editorial Assistant at Routledge, Rhea Gupta, and Sarah Hyde, the Editor (Routledge Education), for the guidance and support through the various stages of the book.

We are indebted to all our colleagues and friends for sharing the honest accounts of the micro-moments, the 'ahaa' moments, that helped shape them into learning and teaching leaders. We would like to express our collective appreciation to J'annine Jobling for her helpful comments on the final draft of the manuscript. In addition, we are grateful for the funding from Liverpool Hope University that supported the proofreading for the volume. We must each say a special thank you to our families for their patience and support as we pursued our intellectual project.

Part I
Introduction

1 Teaching and learning leadership in higher education

An introduction

Josephine Lang and Anesa Hosein

Introduction

Over the years, the prestige of research leadership has overshadowed teaching and learning leadership in academia (Hosein et al., 2023; Rao et al., 2023). However, in recent times, several attempts have been made to engage with scholarship and leadership in teaching and learning in ways which may be parallel to research leadership. The discipline of Scholarship of Teaching and Learning (SoTL) has gained significance and become well-established in recent times, particularly since Ernest Boyer's book *Scholarship Reconsidered: Priorities of the Professoriate* (1990), with its challenge to make the status of quality teaching, supported by its scholarship, equal with traditional research activity in higher education. A significant illustration of engaging the SoTL discipline for action in a higher education context is the Carnegie Foundation report (Huber & Hutchings, 2005), which, among other themes, highlighted the need to establish new organisational structures to foster communities and commons for teaching and learning – as well as raising the role that students may play in this scholarship. Further, the SoTL special issue of the *Higher Education Research and Development* journal (Vardi, 2011) examines the changes in the higher education landscape since Boyer's SoTL model emerged, with new challenges and implications for the sector. More recently, Michael Houdyshell and his colleagues published their findings about their faculty's engagement with Boyer's model through the establishment of a Professional Learning Community (Houdyshell et al., 2022). The inquiry delved into the faculty's understandings of Boyer's model as well as the functioning of the Professional Learning Community, particularly to foster scholarship in teaching. The report uncovered some of the challenges embodied in aspects of Boyer's model, relating to teaching scholarship in a climate of competing priorities. Yet the team acknowledged that some of the identified challenges may have been the consequence of the way the leader implemented the Professional Learning Community.

In contrast, research in the discipline of teaching and learning leadership is much sparser and seems not to have such a significant foothold in the research literature as its underpinning discipline of SoTL. For example, in Maryellen Weimer's (2006) *Enhancing Scholarly Work on Teaching and Learning*, only the final chapter (Chapter 9) has advice for academic leaders to foster a culture of SoTL in their institutions. Weimer outlines three features for a leadership agenda to encourage a culture of *pedagogical scholarship* (her term):

- *Breadth* – develop organisational structures and processes that support the wide range of pedagogic scholarship and its recognition;
- *Creative, Innovative and Open* – to be inclusive of new and creative definitions and approaches to pedagogic scholarship that can be discipline specific, rather than generic;
- *Positive* – that the motivation for doing the scholarly practice is for reasons of valuing teaching and gaining greater recognition for teaching as scholarly work, rather than pursuing it solely to improve, which is often accompanied with derogatory tones.

Similarly, while Peter Knight and Paul Trowler's (2001) book focuses on leadership in higher education, it too has only one chapter dedicated to leading teaching and learning (see Chapter 6). The chapter initially centres on learning propositions and then moves to identifying implications for leaders, including the challenges of leading on a teaching and learning agenda, particularly because good learning takes time to plan and implement. Peculiarly, Knight and Trowler concede that for a 'new head of department wanting to make an impact it might be easier to start with improving the research effort' (2001, p. 118). Bruce Macfarlane (2011, 2012) offers more hope as he positions the professoriate as important resources in the modern university sector. He argues that intellectual leadership embodies two dimensions of the work and life of the professor, which are academic freedom and academic duty, leading to four orientations: academic citizen, public intellectual, knowledge producer and boundary transgressor (Macfarlane, 2012, pp. 110–111). But again, the discussion is broad and is not applied specifically to teaching and learning leadership. In the descriptive self-narrative of her case study, Claire Taylor (2019) discusses her application of a school-based *Learning without Limits* model to develop the *Leading without Limits* model in her faculty as their leader. Her re-purposing of the transformative model for leadership is underpinned by three principles that are (i) co-agency, (ii) everybody, and (iii) trust. These principles are based on a reflective practice and reflexivity approach. Taylor's case study examined the re-purposed model to guide her leadership behaviours in the implementation of a distributed approach to academic development. Initial findings seem to support that the re-purposed model may deliver on a leadership of change in academic development contexts.

Considering the paucity of literature on leadership in teaching and learning, this book brings together examples of teaching and learning critical incidents from England and Australia which the pedagogic leaders (chapter contributors of this book) have identified as pivotal in establishing them as such leaders.

Why case studies?

In this book, we focus on case studies to provide tangible and in-depth stories of how leadership occurs within teaching and learning. The book draws on case studies from Australia and the UK to provide a comparative understanding of how leadership in learning and teaching is evolving, being recognised and being valued in two different national systems. Each of the case studies shared in Part II is bounded by the experience as lived by an academic or professional staff member within the higher education sector in their becoming or being a teaching and learning leader. Owing to the highly contextualised case description, the chapters provide an interpretation within the context of the lived experience of the authors. As argued by Merriam (1988), the 'case study seeks holistic description and explanation' (p. 10) of the phenomenon. Some of the book chapter cases may be categorised as a *descriptive case study* in that they richly describe the author's lived experience of an incident which helped establish their teaching and learning leadership. Often, descriptive case studies are used to build knowledge foundations in areas of education that are little researched (Merriam, 1988). Thus, it makes sense that some of the book's chapters offer a descriptive case study approach (e.g. refer to Jasvir Kaur Nachatar Singh's or Lucie Zundans-Fraser's chapters) as the teaching and learning leadership research is currently limited. However, some case studies within the book could be better categorised as an illustration of an *interpretive case study*. While interpretive case studies are richly descriptive, they also engage in using the case study data with the intention to interpret or theorise the phenomenon and there is a 'level of abstraction and conceptualisation in interpretive cases studies [that] may range from suggesting relationships among variables to constructing theory' (Merriam, 1988, p. 28). Illustrations of book chapters adhering to the principles of interpretive case study approaches include the chapters by Duncan Lawson and Barbie Panther, where they have drawn on existing theoretical frameworks to analyse their own lived experiences of incidents which helped establish their teaching and learning leadership.

The power of narratives

Regardless of the types of case studies that are presented in Part II – all are expressions of storytelling by the authors of the critical incidents (Tripp, 1993) that established their teaching and learning leadership in higher education.

The storytelling and analysis associated with identifying critical incidents are acts of reflexivity. As David Tripp explains:

> Incidents happen, but critical incidents are produced by the way we look at a situation: a critical incident is an interpretation of the significance of an event. To take something as a critical incident is a value judgement we make, and the basis of that judgement is the significance we attach to the meaning of the incident.
>
> (1993, p. 8)

Therefore, these chapters are not only cases, but foremost they are narratives. Fundamentally, people make sense of their world through sharing stories of incidents; narrative structures are at the core of being human (Hanne & Kaal, 2019). As argued by Jerome Bruner, there are two modes of thought that work complementarily to each other and both are important 'to capture the rich diversity of thought' – one is reasoning, and the other is narrative (Bruner, 1986, p. 11). This *narrative knowing* is constructed 'through the stories we tell about lived experience that help make sense of the complexity and ambiguity of human existence' (Hanne & Kaal, 2019, p. 5). In fact, it is argued that the only way of 'describing *lived time* . . . is in the form of narrative' as we construct ourselves autobiographically in story telling (Bruner, 2004, p. 692). Hence, the chapter authors in Part II describe their lived time and incidents in the form of their autobiographical narratives. In doing so, the authors are reflexively examining their significant life moments to share incidents that are critical to their teaching and learning leadership development. While there may be contestations about the veracity or integrity of storytelling, Bruner (2004) argues that there are cultural conventions and language usage that inform the act of life narrative construction, which mitigate the dilemma of judging the narrative's rightness. Hence, 'life narratives achieve the power to structure perceptual experience, to organize memory, to segment and purpose-build the very "events" of a life. In the end, we *become* the autobiographical narratives by which we "tell about" our lives' (Bruner, 2004, p. 694). Thus, narratives (and its sister conceptual tool, the metaphor) are 'framing devices' that can illuminate or conceal events, but, undoubtedly, they help to unpack the complexity of phenomena through the selection of elements that are shared in the telling of the narrative or metaphor (Hanne & Kaal, 2019, p. 6). Often, 'reflexivity and narrative are . . . bracketed together' because it is in the act of retrospection that meaning is assigned and generated to the significance of the lived experience that contributes to the sharing of the narrative (Trahar, 2006, p. 16). In other words, 'we build meanings by working with experience' that are contextualised or in 'relationship' with past and present experiences to inform our future knowing and practices (Moon, 2004, p. 21). Hence, 'meaning is not present or absent' in experience; rather, it is achieved by the reflective learner/practitioner to draw out the 'meaning relevant to the context' of that experience being captured in the story (Moon, 2006, p. 23).

In sharing their self-narratives of teaching and learning leadership incidents, the authors are the story tellers and you, the readers, become the listeners – suggesting a collaboration for sense-making (Trahar, 2006). Each author explores the phenomenon from within their unique context of their lived experience. As they reflect on incidents critical to establishing their teaching and learning leadership, they have already engaged in making meaning of their lifeworld(s). As academic leaders they are sense-making, which is at the 'heart of leadership, and it is particularly important in the complex and confusing world of higher education' (Gallos & Bolman, 2021, p. 33). In the event sense-making reveals misinterpretation that led to failure, Gallos and Bolman (2021) challenges leaders to 'reframe: to examine the world from alternative perspectives, seeking new ways to understand and new strategies to move ahead' (p. 33). In the act of sharing their narratives of the leadership with you, the reader/listener, you will bring your own interpretation to their stories, and as editors, we invite you to bring further colour to their reflective description and analysis with your own contexts. What are you learning from these stories as cases to contribute to your own worldmaking (Goodman, 1978) in teaching and learning leadership?

The structure of the book

The book consists of three parts:

Part I: Introduction
Part II: Case studies on teaching and learning leadership
Part III: Implications for practice.

Outline of Part II – the case studies

Part II presents the key focus of the book that captures how teaching and learning leaders within higher education use case studies to tell their stories about leadership and the lessons they have learned (see Table 1.1). In sharing the critical incidents of their teaching and learning leadership, they are contributing to documenting the empirical evidence of the work of this academic leadership in universities, which has been identified as sorely lacking in this specialist area of leadership (e.g. Scott et al., 2008).

The seven case studies shared in Part II frequently used theories of leadership and, in some cases, theories of educational leadership to provide frameworks of analysis to deepen the author's reflections with the aim to increase transferability to other higher education contexts for teaching and learning leadership. Some authors (such as Gita Sedghi, Lucia Zudans-Fraser and Jasvir Kaur Nachatar Singh) chose a more holistic approach to their narrative-telling and reflected on key incidents across their life, demonstrating how they align within their particular case study. Other authors (e.g. Duncan Lawson and Josephine Lang) chose to showcase the work of teaching and learning leadership through one or two significant episodes to examine key characteristics of this type of leadership. In contrast, Silvia Colaiacome and her colleague reflect on their co-leadership in teaching and learning and, through their narrative-sharing, raise the issue of collaboration in leadership to enhance student learning. Finally, Barbie Panther shares her teaching and learning leadership through the lens of a quest metaphor. Together, this compendium of narratives bestows a gift to the higher education sector of how learning and teaching leadership may be represented and reflects diversity and complexity. A summary of each chapter is given in Table 1.1.

Duncan Lawson discusses in his chapter his teaching and learning leadership development through the establishment of a centre (**sigma**) to support higher education students with statistics and mathematics across disciplines. He argues that he used a 'pragmatic leadership' (Mumford & Van Doorn, 2001) approach to establishing and sustaining the centre, which celebrated 30 years of mathematics and statistics support in 2021, as well as leading an emerging national network of similar centres that support student learning.

Gita Sedghi focuses on leadership that creates inclusive and transformative learning for students. She considers the challenges of teaching and learning leadership and calls for institutional recognition of distributed leadership approaches, particularly in creating and leading positive learning experiences for her students via the peer-assisted learning initiative. As such, Gita concludes on the importance of building capability towards teaching and learning leadership through a relational perspective that is underpinned by influence

Table 1.1 Leadership case studies

Chapter	Author	Country	Case Study
Chapter 2	Duncan Lawson	UK	Pragmatic leadership for collaboration in a competitive sector: The case of sigma
Chapter 3	Gita Sedghi	UK	Leading for inclusivity: Peer-assisted learning and internationalisation
Chapter 4	Lucia Zundans-Fraser	Australia	Stepping stones towards higher education teaching and learning leadership: A case study on becoming a Deputy Dean
Chapter 5	Silvia Colaiacomo and Tom Sharp	UK	Opportunities and barriers to leadership in student support services: A case study of inclusive assessment
Chapter 6	Josephine Lang	Australia	Be(com)ing an academic leader: A case study on a collaborative partnership for external peer review
Chapter 7	Jasvir Kaur Nachatar Singh	Australia	Leading as an international academic: A case study of a casual teaching team
Chapter 8	Barbara C. Panther	Australia	A leadership quest in teaching and learning: A case study of building capability and competency

and inspiration, rather than gained through authoritative responsibility of a formal leadership position.

Lucie Zundans-Fraser reflectively examines her pathway to having the leadership position of Deputy Dean. She explores the multi-faceted roles of being a Deputy Dean as well as unpacking the complex factors that contribute to her academic leadership. She discusses significant moments that 'punctuate' her teaching and learning leadership development and shape her leadership identity and experience.

Silvia Colaiacomo along with her colleague Tom Sharp from professional services discuss in their contribution, teaching and learning leadership within the services that support higher education students. Silvia Colaiacomo, from the perspective of an academic, and Tom Sharp, from the perspective of a professional staff, deliberate the opportunities and challenges of delivering quality support, particularly for students with disabilities in a complex system that interacts between professional staff, academics and students. They argue for system change that shifts towards leadership based on a humanist approach and shares responsibilities to support and enhance the learning experience for students with disabilities.

Josephine Lang applies Juntrasook's (2014) four categories of leadership meanings to analyse collaborative leadership in academia using her case study of external peer review. Through this, she reflects on her leadership of significant roles or responsibilities with the view to unpack the complexities of being a leader for teaching and learning in higher education. The examination suggests that the four categories are intertwined and contribute unique characteristics to the becoming of, and being, a leader for teaching and learning.

Jasvir Kaur Nachatar Singh presents numerous factors that shape the teaching and learning context in the higher education sector from the perspective of an international student becoming an academic in her host country. Through her lived experience, she examines the multiple differences of the higher education systems between Malaysia and Australia and focuses on her interactions with the casual teaching staff. She reflects on how she identifies, negotiates and adapts to those cultural differences to inform her leadership practice when working with the casual staff to enhance the quality of the learning experience for students.

Leaders in higher education have the interests of a multitude of stakeholders to consider, influence and impact, and these interests change as the scope of leadership roles evolves. Barbie Panther uses a quest metaphor to richly describe her evolving teaching and learning leadership approach by reflecting on critical moments to draw out lessons learned by looking at the case of enhancing leadership capabilities and competences. Furthermore, she uses Scott et al.'s (2008) academic leadership model and its capability framework as a basis for reflection on the changing capabilities and competencies required as she took on more senior educational leadership roles, both formal and informal, and the types of professional development she sought to support these changes.

Finally, in Part III, the last chapter draws upon the case studies represented to provide a summative analysis of the learning from the shared lived experiences of teaching and learning leadership as articulated by the critical incidents shared as case studies by the contributors. This reflective analysis identifies insights across the cases to inform the higher education sector to consider strategies to actively support academics and professional staff to undertake the transition to be leaders for teaching and learning.

References

Boyer, E. L. (1990). *Scholarship reconsidered: Priorities of the professoriate*. Carnegie Foundation for the Advancement of Teaching.
Bruner, J. (1986). *Actual minds, possible worlds*. Harvard University Press.
Bruner, J. (2004). Life as narrative. *Social Research, 71*(3), 691–710.
Gallos, J. V., & Bolman, L. G. (2021). *Reframing academic leadership* (2nd ed.). Jossey-Bass.
Goodman, N. (1978). *Ways of worldmaking*. Hackett Publishing Company.
Hanne, M., & Kaal, A. A. (Eds.). (2019). *Narrative and metaphor in education: Look both ways*. Routledge.
Hosein, A., Rao, N., & Kinchin, I. (2023). *Narratives of becoming leaders in disciplinary and institutional contexts: Leadership identity in learning and teaching in higher education*. London Bloomsbury.
Houdyshell, M., Sughrue, J., Carothers, D., & Aydin, H. (2022). Is Boyer's scholarship reconsidered still relevant: A case study of a college-wide professional learning community. *Journal of the Scholarship of Teaching and Learning, 22*(1), 113–137. doi:10.14434/josotl.v22i1.31185
Huber, M. T., & Hutchings, P. (2005). *The advancement of learning: Building the teaching commons*. The Carnegie Foundation for the Advancement of Teaching and Josey-Bass.
Juntrasook, A. (2014). 'You do not have to be the boss to be a leader': contested meanings of leadership in higher education. *Higher Education Research & Development, 33*(1), 19–31. doi: 10.1080/07294360.2013.864610
Knight, P. T., & Trowler, P. R. (2001). *Departmental leadership in higher education*. The Society for Research into Higher Education & Open University Press.
Macfarlane, B. (2011). Professors as intellectual leaders: Formation, identity and role. *Studies in Higher Education, 36*(1), 57–73.
Macfarlane, B. (2012). *Intellectual leadership in higher education: Renewing the role of the university professor*. Routledge.
Merriam, S. B. (1988). *Case study research in education: A qualitative approach*. Jossey-Bass Publishers.
Moon, J. (2004). *A handbook of reflective and experiential learning: Theory and practice*. Routledge Falmer.
Moon, J. (2006). *Learning journals: A handbook for reflective practice and professional development* (2nd ed.). Routledge.
Mumford, M. D., & Van Doorn, J. R. (2001). The leadership of pragmatism: Reconsidering Franklin in the age of charisma. *The Leadership Quarterly, 12*(3), 279–309.

Rao, N., Hosein, A., & Kinchin, I. (2023). *Narratives of academics' personal journeys in contested spaces: Leadership identity in learning and teaching in higher education.* Bloomsbury.

Scott, G., Coates, H., & Anderson, M. (2008). *Learning leaders in times of change: Academic leadership capabilities for Australian higher education.* Camberwell, VIC. https://research.acer.edu.au/cgi/viewcontent.cgi?article=1001&context=higher_education

Taylor, C. (2019). From learning without limits to leading without limits: An autobiographical reflective case study of leading academic development within higher education. *Innovations in Education and Teaching International, 56*(6), 679–689.

Trahar, S. (Ed.). (2006). *Narrative research on learning: Comparative and international perspectives.* Symposium Books.

Tripp, D. (1993). *Critical incidents in teaching: Developing professional judgement.* Routledge.

Vardi, I. (2011). The changing relationship between the scholarship of teaching (and learning) and universities. *Higher Education Research & Development, 30*(1), 1–7.

Weimer, M. (2006). *Enhancing scholarly work on teaching and learning: Professional literature that makes a difference.* Jossey-Bass.

Part II
Case studies on teaching and learning leadership

2 Pragmatic leadership for collaboration in a competitive sector

The case of sigma

Duncan Lawson

Introduction: my career and values

I am currently in my second term as Director of *sigma*, the mathematics and statistics support service at Coventry University. During my career, I have held a wide variety of roles including Director of the Mathematics, Statistics and Operations Research subject centre of the Higher Education Academy (now Advance HE) and Pro-Vice-Chancellor (Formative Education) at Newman University in Birmingham. This case study focuses on my academic leadership of the development of mathematics and statistics support across the higher education sector in the UK.

My career-long involvement with mathematics and statistics support and my approach to academic leadership have been motivated and informed by some key beliefs and values:

- I regard higher education as a public good (Filippakou & Williams, 2015);
- I strongly support widening participation (see, e.g. Blunkett, 1998);
- I am convinced that universities, since they control their own admissions, have a responsibility to their students to provide appropriate opportunities for individual success;
- I disagree with the UK government policy of ever-increased marketisation of higher education (Nixon et al., 2010);
- I believe that students are better served by collaboration between institutions rather than by the excessive competition that results from this marketisation.

Mathematics and statistics support

Mathematics and statistics support is an academic service that is provided in recognition of the fact that students of many disciplines (e.g. engineering, economics, political science, psychology nursing) require some mathematical or statistical skills to succeed in their studies. Furthermore, many students arrive at university under-prepared for the mathematical demands of their course. According to the Advisory Committee on Mathematics Education:

> We estimate that of those entering higher education each year, some 330,000 would benefit from recent experience of studying some mathematics (including statistics) at a level beyond GCSE, but fewer than 125,000 have done so.
>
> (ACME, 2011, p. 1)

This statement alone provides a rationale for providing mathematics support; however, a fuller rationale is set out in Croft et al. (2016, p. 2).

In 1990, Coventry Polytechnic established the BP Mathematics Centre, one of the first formal, large-scale mathematics support provisions in the UK (Lawson, 2021). From its inception, I was involved with the centre, becoming its director in 1993. Although the title was somewhat grander than the role itself, this was my first experience of academic leadership. It was not a position that I applied for; instead, it was something my Head of Department asked me to do – perhaps because he saw leadership potential in me, or perhaps because he had to find someone to take on the role. Whatever the reason, this presented me with an opportunity to develop gradually as a leader in an area of academia that resonated strongly with many of my personal values and beliefs. Throughout my career since then, I have continued to contribute to mathematics support through teaching, research and policy development.

Mathematics support during the 1990s has been described as a Cinderella service (Grove et al., 2018) and a 'form of cottage industry practised by a few well meaning, possibly eccentric individuals' (Kyle, 2010, p. 103). However, since then things have progressed, and mathematics and statistics support provisions are now firmly embedded in the academic support infrastructure of the overwhelming majority of institutions in the UK, Ireland, Australia and in a growing number of institutions in countries such as Germany, Czech Republic and Norway (Lawson et al., 2020).

A major milestone on this journey from the fringes to the mainstream was the success, in 2005, of a joint bid from Loughborough and Coventry Universities represented by Tony Croft and me, respectively,[1] to the Higher Education Funding Council for England's (HEFCE) Centres for Excellence in Teaching and Learning (CETL) programme. This bid was based around our joint expertise in mathematics support and led to the establishment of *sigma*, whose sub-title was 'Centre for Excellence in university-wide mathematics and statistics support'. At this time, the mathematics support provision at both Loughborough and Coventry Universities was well-established and reasonably funded. Our motivation in applying for the status and funding of a CETL was both to improve the service in our own institutions and to expand mathematics support provision across the sector for the benefit of as many students as possible.

Being a CETL gave not only status but also access to very large sums of money – a large CETL (such as *sigma*) received £2 million of capital funding at the outset and annual revenue of £0.5 million over five years. The CETL programme was HEFCE's largest-ever individual programme for improving teaching and learning; its total budget was £315 million. The intention had been for this programme to have a significant impact on learning and teaching in the sector. However, in final evaluations of HEFCE's CETL scheme (SQW, 2011; Ramsden, 2012), lack of benefit beyond CETL host institutions was one of the major criticisms. The CETL programme ended in 2010 and *sigma* is one of only a small number of the 70+ HEFCE-funded CETLs that still has a visible presence in the UK's university sector.

The importance of collaboration

A major factor in the longevity of *sigma* has been our focus on collaboration. From the outset, we determined that *sigma* should be a centre **FOR** excellence rather than a centre **OF** excellence. A centre for excellence is one that seeks to identify and promote excellence wherever it is found, whilst a centre of excellence presents what it does as excellence and (possibly) seeks to share that with others. To this end, we gave substantial amounts of *sigma*'s CETL funding to support activity in other institutions. This money was used in various ways, including:

- to establish mathematics support at institutions that had no such provision;
- for secondment projects to enable staff working at other institutions to collaborate with colleagues within *sigma* on projects to develop resources that could be used at institutions across the sector;
- to fund a mentoring programme where experienced practitioners from one institution would support novice practitioners at another;
- to provide professional development workshops for those working in mathematics and statistics support;
- to establish regional hubs, where those involved in the provision of mathematics support could meet (both informally and formally) with colleagues from nearby institutions to share experiences, problems and (hopefully) solutions;
- to hold an annual, subsidised conference.

The focus of all these schemes was capacity and community building. Whilst Loughborough and Coventry Universities had sizeable mathematics and statistics support provision, each with several members of staff involved, in newly established provisions in other institutions there was often only one member of staff. There were two common scenarios. Firstly, mathematics support was provided by a mathematics department where most staff were research-focused, and one teaching-focused individual was given the responsibility for mathematics support. Secondly, mathematics support was provided as part of a broad institutional academic support unit and, within this unit, a single person had responsibility for mathematics support. We saw the development of community as a way to combat the isolation of these individuals, providing opportunities for interaction with others in a similar position to themselves. Furthermore, we recognised that the generous financial grants of the CETL years would not last forever and that, when there was no longer any funding, we needed to have established a critical mass of practitioners who had learned from first-hand experience the benefits of collaborating within a community of practice (Wenger, 1998) and so would continue to work together.

For a combination of reasons, of which our outward-looking focus was almost certainly the most important, *sigma* secured further substantial funding from the National Higher Education STEM Programme (2009–12) in the UK and then from HEFCE's Strategically Important Vulnerable Subjects (SIVS) fund (2013–16) to continue the development of mathematics and statistics support and the establishment of a sustainable practitioner community. During the period 2005–16, *sigma* directly assisted (through provision of finance and expertise) the establishment of mathematics and statistics support provision at 36 higher education institutions throughout England and Wales. We also initiated the sigma-Network,[2] a voluntary association of mathematics and statistics support practitioners which remains active to this day.

Pragmatic leadership tinged with servant leadership

The title of this case study highlights 'pragmatic leadership' (Mumford & Van Doorn, 2001) since we were attempting to promote collaboration in a sector where competition was increasingly becoming the dominant ethos. We did so not by compromising our values, but by being analytic about how best to achieve our goals in the environment in which we found ourselves. Pragmatic leadership is characterised by a focus on practical problems and 'the need for solution rather than identity and personal meaning' (Mumford & Van Doorn, 2001, p. 282). To this end, we were more than willing to harness support wherever we found it.

For example, David Willetts (then Minister of State for Universities and Science) and a strong proponent of the marketisation of higher education (DBIS, 2011) became one of *sigma*'s staunchest supporters (see Willetts, 2013, p. 51). During a visit to Loughborough University, the minister was taken to the Mathematics Learning Support Centre and immediately recognised its value to students within the institution. After this, he began to praise mathematics support in speeches. His support was because our work made a difference to student outcomes rather than because it was a collaborative endeavour between institutions. Nonetheless, it is likely that his support was influential in *sigma* securing SIVS funding in 2013.

Likewise, we were aware that senior management within our own institutions wished to gain a competitive edge from hosting a CETL. So, we maintained direct channels of communication with these managers, informing them of our successes (such as the Times Higher Education Award for Outstanding Support for Students in 2011) and presenting ourselves as the leading institutions in a field of increasing importance. This gave them material that could be used in their institutional publicity whilst enabling us to pursue our collaborative agenda. However, we were aware that there were limits to how much we could use institutional funding for initiatives that were essentially sector-wide, and, indeed, it would be improper to do so to any significant extent. Therefore, it was important to secure external funding: it increased our standing with our local senior management since substantial grants are always welcome in universities, and it gave us a measure of independence to pursue our collaborative agenda. We were careful to ensure that the terms of the follow-on funding from HE-STEM and HEFCE SIVS made clear that a key purpose of the funding was the development of the mathematics and statistics support community across the whole sector, since this inter-institutional collaboration was, in our opinion, critical to the sustainability of the provision.

Although we were not aware of leadership models at the time, post hoc exploration of leadership approaches firmly aligns our practice as pragmatic rather than charismatic or ideological (Mumford et al., 2008). A key characteristic of pragmatic leadership which we would recognise in ourselves is 'these leaders will prefer logical argumentation to emotionally evocative arguments. These arguments, moreover, will not be framed to appeal to people in general but rather to knowledgeable elites who understand and can induce control, over relevant causes and contingencies' (Mumford et al., 2008, p. 147). We understood that whilst creating a community of mathematics and statistics support practitioners was vitally important, the effectiveness of these practitioners would always be dependent on local circumstances and the support (or otherwise) of senior managers.

For this reason, we ensured that we provided information and resources not only to our own senior managers (as mentioned above) but also to senior managers across the sector. We undertook a research project (Mackenzie et al., 2016) which involved interviewing senior managers with responsibility for learning and teaching, typically Pro-Vice-Chancellors, about their understanding of the mathematical and statistical needs of all their students (not just those taking STEM courses). We prepared a guide for Pro-Vice-Chancellors about the oversight of mathematics support (Croft et al., 2016) and sent this to the Pro-Vice-Chancellor responsible for learning and teaching at every UK university. This guide not only covered good practice in the provision of mathematics support but also showed how such support could impact on such things as retention rates, employability, National Student Survey results and Teaching Excellence Framework outcomes – all issues that were highly important to Pro-Vice-Chancellors.

We had learned from many years' experience that achieving senior management support is essential for the long-term sustainability of mathematics support provision within an institution, since it is a service that consumes budget but does not directly generate income. When distributing funding from the HE-STEM and SIVS grants to institutions to establish or enhance mathematics support provision, we designed the success criteria to assist new mathematics support provisions to secure this senior management support. The funding was allocated through a competitive bidding process in which institutions were required to commit to match (with their own funds) the income received from *sigma* over the duration of the award, typically a two-year period, with quarterly reporting. If institutional funding had not been forthcoming, then the next quarter's *sigma* funding would be withheld. In practice, this situation never arose. Furthermore, at the point of submitting the bid, an institutional senior manager had to submit a letter of support in which they committed to continue the provision for at least a further two years after the end of *sigma* funding. In reality, we had no way of enforcing this commitment. However, the overwhelming majority of mathematics support provisions that *sigma* funding helped to establish are still operational today.

The focus of our analysis of leadership models that apply to our practice has been on pragmatic leadership. However, it is also worth noting that we identify elements of servant leadership (Greenleaf, 1977) in our practice. Spears (2002) identified ten characteristics of servant leadership, and, of these, we would identify at least six (i.e. listening, awareness, persuasion, conceptualisation, commitment to the growth of people and building community) as significant in our own practice. Listening, awareness, persuasion and conceptualisation overlap significantly with the behaviours of pragmatic leaders but commitment to the growth of people and building community are not necessarily features of pragmatic leadership. They do however resonate with our belief in collaboration as a productive approach. Furthermore, 'servant leaders are ethical' (Northouse, 2016, p. 225), and it is our ethical beliefs and values, such as those outlined in the introduction, that have provided a strong direction to the work we have undertaken.

Conclusions

Pragmatic leadership seems well-suited for academia as it tends to rely on logical argument rather than emotional appeal. However, it does also rely on the leader's expertise in problem analysis and determination of feasible solutions and the means to achieve them. As such, pragmatic leaders may be open to charges from ideologues of abandoning their principles and of settling for second-rate compromises. Pragmatic leadership requires a balancing of the lofty aspirations of peers and the (sometimes) different agendas of 'elites'. This is not to say that pragmatic leadership is amoral. We have been able to stay true to our beliefs, particularly in the value of inter-institutional collaboration rather than competition. Our values have been enabled, not compromised, by a pragmatic leadership approach.

Pragmatic leadership has enabled us to develop a sustainable voluntary collaborative community of mathematics and statistics support professionals by effective 'managing up' of university and political leaders. This 'managing up' has included ensuring that they are aware of the contribution that mathematics and statistics support can make to their areas of responsibility and to external measures by which higher education quality is judged. These senior leaders do not have to be supportive of mathematics and statistics support for its own sake – it is fine for them to appreciate its value in terms of the effect it has on things that matter to them.

Listening and awareness are behaviours identified in both pragmatic and servant leaders. These are particularly important in the mathematics and statistics support community. Members of this community tend to be values-driven, have deep commitment to their students and believe in the transformative potential of education. They can also sometimes feel overlooked in terms of reward and recognition. Listening to their concerns and providing opportunities for their personal and professional development have empowered the collaborative community to not be dependent on its two founders. Empowering actions have included a 'Developing the next generation of leaders' workshop, relaunching the journal *MSOR Connections*[3] as a vehicle for their practice-based publications, acting as a referee in support of promotion applications and stepping aside from national roles to allow opportunities for others. It is important that the style of leadership has matched the values and characteristics of the mathematics and statistics support community. Research by Liden and his co-workers has shown that servant leadership has a positive impact on performance where this caring, empowering leadership style is valued by the community in which it is exercised, but not so in organisations where this approach is not respected (see, e.g. Liden, Wayne et al., 2008).

Mumford et al. (2008, p. 147) suggested that 'pragmatic leaders were more likely to build lasting institutions and charismatic leaders were more likely to initiate mass movements'. It is our hope that the mathematics and statistics support centres that have been developed across the country will be 'lasting institutions' that enable many hundreds of thousands of students to better manage the mathematical and statistical demands of their studies, to achieve their full potential and to emerge from university well-prepared for the quantitative demands of their roles in society.

Notes

1 Tony Croft and I became Directors of the CETL which was called *sigma*. Hereafter in this case study, 'we' will be used to refer to the two of us as we worked closely together and shared key values regarding the importance of collaboration and of expanding mathematics and statistics support across the sector for the benefit of all students.

2 www.sigma-network.ac.uk
3 https://journals.gre.ac.uk/index.php/msor

References

ACME. (2011). *Mathematical needs: Mathematics in the workplace and in higher education*. The Royal Society. https://royalsociety.org/-/media/policy/Publications/2011/mathematical-needs-mathematics-in-the-workplace-and-in-higher-education-06-2017.pdf

Blunkett, D. (1998). *The learning age: A renaissance for a new Britain*. The Stationery Office. www.educationengland.org.uk/documents/gp1998b/index.html

Croft, T., Grove, M., & Lawson, D. (2016). *The oversight of mathematics, statistics and numeracy support provision at university level: A guide for pro-vice-chancellors*. Sigma Network. www.sigma-network.ac.uk/wp-content/uploads/2016/10/66141-Senior-Management-Handbook-AWK-WEB.pdf

DBIS [Department of Business, Innovation and Skills]. (2011). *Higher education: Students at the heart of the system* (Cm 8122). The Stationery Office. https://assets.publishing.service.gov.uk/government/uploads/system/uploads/attachment_data/file/31384/11-944-higher-education-students-at-heart-of-system.pdf

Filippakou, O., & Williams, G. (2015). *Higher education as a public good: Critical perspectives on theory, policy and practice*. Peter Lang.

Greenleaf, R. (1977). *Servant leadership: A journey into the nature of legitimate power and greatness*. Paulist Press.

Grove, M. J., Brown, G., Croft, A. C., Hibberd, S., Levesley, J., & Linton, C. (2018). Where next for mathematics education in higher education? *MSOR Connections*, *16*(2), 3–15. https://doi.org/10.21100/msor.v16i2.777

Kyle, J. (2010). Affordability, adaptability, approachability and sustainability. In C. M. Marr & M. J. Grove (Eds.), *Responding to the mathematics problem* (pp. 103–104). Maths, Stats & OR Network. www.mathcentre.ac.uk/resources/uploaded/mathssupport volumefinal.pdf

Lawson, D. (2021). A history of the development of the mathematics and statistics support community in the United Kingdom. Part 1: From alpha to sigma. *MSOR Connections*, *19*(1), 5–12. https://doi.org/10.21100/msor.v19i1.1118

Lawson, D., Grove, M., & Croft, T. (2020). The evolution of mathematics support: A literature review. *International Journal of Mathematical Education in Science and Technology*, *51*(8), 1224–1254. https://doi.org/10.1080/0020739X.2019.1662120

Liden, R. C., Wayne, S. J., Zhao, H., & Henderson, D. (2008). Servant leadership: Development of a multidimensional measure and multi-level assessment. *Leadership Quarterly*, *19*, 161–177.

Mackenzie, H., Tolley, H., Croft, T., Grove, M., & Lawson, D. (2016). Senior management perspectives of mathematics and statistics support in higher education: Moving to an 'ecological' approach'. *Journal of Higher Education Policy and Management*, *38*(5), 550–561.

Mumford, M. D., Antes, A. L., Caughron, J. J., & Friedrich, T. L. (2008). Charismatic, ideological, and pragmatic leadership: Multi-level influences on emergence and performance. *The Leadership Quarterly*, *19*(2), 144–160. https://doi.org/10.1016/j.leaqua.2008.01.002

Mumford, M. D., & Van Doorn, J. R. (2001). The leadership of pragmatism: Reconsidering Franklin in the age of charisma. *The Leadership Quarterly, 12*(3), 279–309. https://doi.org/10.1016/S1048-9843(01)00080-7

Nixon, E., Molesworth, M., & Scullion, R. (Eds.). (2010). *The marketisation of higher education and the student as consumer*. Routledge.

Northouse, P. G. (2016). *Leadership: Theory and practice* (7th ed.). Sage.

Ramsden, P. (2012). A poor policy, poorly managed leaves little to show for £315m. *Times Higher Education*, 15 March, 32–33.

Spears, L. C. (2002). Tracing the past, present and future of servant leadership. In L. C. Spears & M. Lawrence (Eds.), *Focus on leadership: Servant-leadership for the 21st century* (pp. 1–16). Wiley.

SQW. (2011). *Summative evaluation of the CETL programme. Final report by SQW to HEFCE and DEL*. https://dera.ioe.ac.uk/13215/1/rd11_11.pdf

Wenger, E. (1998). *Communities of practice: Learning, meaning and identity*. Cambridge University Press.

Willetts, D. (2013). *Robbins revisited: Bigger and better higher education*. The Social Market Foundation. www.smf.co.uk/wp-content/uploads/2013/10/Publication-Robbins-Revisited-Bigger-and-Better-Higher-Education-David-Willetts.pdf

3 Leading for inclusivity

Peer-assisted learning and internationalisation

Gita Sedghi

I will explain a series of negative and positive experiences behind these success stories to help higher education educators to enhance their leadership by reflecting on their work, learning from experiences and moving on positively to reach their targets. I will describe how my leadership skills in learning and teaching, including influencing change, clear vision, communication, inclusivity, networking and resilience, were shaped through this journey. The key themes of the case studies include unpacking the values of student-staff partnerships, starting an initiative at small scale, student voice and evidence-informed practice – and how these values can upscale teaching and learning projects.

Introduction

Providing inclusive learning and teaching in higher education for a diverse community of students is an integral part of my role as an educator. My passion for inclusive education has been nourished partly by my personal experiences of studying as a mature international student with a young child and establishing a career in the UK. As an Asian woman teaching chemistry at the University of Liverpool and researching in education, I have put my own experiences of the challenges of accommodating to a new country and educational setting into practice to create a vision to promote inclusive education for a diverse community of students. Encouraging peer-assisted learning and internationalisation has been central to my efforts in promoting inclusivity within education as a professor of chemistry education.

In this chapter, I will explain how I translated my vision into actions: the journey which enhanced my learning and teaching leadership, including influencing change, clear vision, communication, inclusivity, networking and resilience. The two case studies I present here, which have been central to my development as a leader, show that there is always a series of negative and positive experiences behind each success story. I will demonstrate the challenges, setbacks and successes I experienced. Although I felt disappointed after each setback, I learned from experience and, after reflection, tried a different way to reach my goals. This chapter is my attempt to help higher education educators to enhance their leadership by reflecting on their work, learning from experiences and moving on positively to reach their targets.

Peer-assisted learning for challenging subjects

The Peer-Assisted Learning (PAL) programme provides the first case study in the chapter to examine my teaching and learning leadership. The key themes of this leadership case include unpacking the values of student – staff partnerships, starting an initiative at small scale, student voice and evidence-informed practice – and how these values can upscale teaching and learning projects.

During the academic year 2010/11, there was an increase in the number of Year 1 chemistry students who withdrew from our programmes. As the module leader of the Year 1 Key Skills for Chemists, including general and mathematics skills, I was asked to identify and tackle the underlying issues. I organised student focus groups and interviews to identify the issues and find possible approaches to improve student retention. The student focus groups highlighted the lack of mathematics skills and difficulties in adapting to university life and the programme of study, which affected students' confidence. The transition challenge manifested in an increased number of chemistry students withdrawing from our programmes and a potentially significant barrier to successful student outcomes.

Reviewing scholarly knowledge and practices to tackle the issues arising from the transition from school to university led me to believe that peer-assisted learning was a potential way to develop students' commitment to learning (Hammond et al., 2010) when transitioning to higher education. Peer-assisted learning is student-to-student support where higher year students facilitate study sessions for peers in lower years in the university context (Sedghi, 2019). However, I had no experience setting up such a scheme from scratch, and we did not have a university-level scheme to support academics at the time. After approaching my colleagues to seek advice and support, I was told that some departments at our University had implemented the scheme, but peer-assisted learning had not been sustained in the past. Therefore, at the time, no-one was prepared to invest their time to support my project to design and implement peer-assisted learning. At the same time, as a university teacher, I did not have formal managerial functions that gave me authority or a decision-making role (Liphadzi et al., 2017; Selznick, 1957) to allocate staff and delegate tasks. Hence, I was left with no resources to support my project.

When I encounter barriers, I take a strategic approach to reflective learning by analysing the situation to explore and evaluate alternative routes to reach my destination (Norzailan et al., 2016). Leadership is not always based on formal management positions that give decision-making authority. In fact, my leadership in implementing peer-assisted learning relied on my qualities to influence people to achieve goals (Nikoloski, 2015). Having a strong purpose and a set of values to create an inclusive educational environment for our undergraduate students, I searched for alternative ways to provide myself with resources to design and implement peer-assisted learning. I successfully applied for external funding to implement the scheme locally, which allowed me to review different schemes across the UK to design and tailor peer-assisted learning to the requirements of our students. I chose students as my partners, influenced them to join a working group to design and implement peer-assisted learning, and maintained the team's motivation by developing collective goals and objectives. Therefore, through leading a team of motivated and committed students, I identified an alternative approach to establishing the initiative. Having students as partners from the initial stages of constructing the scheme gave them the ownership of peer-assisted learning, which has been one of the key elements to sustaining it during the past 12 years in the Department of Chemistry (Gravett et al., 2019).

My purpose was to create a sustained scheme, so I was not looking for a quick fix. I strategically started on a small scale and set up peer-assisted learning in my mathematics module, which was one of the most challenging subjects for science students (Shallcross & Yates, 2014). After one semester of delivering the peer-assisted learning sessions, I evaluated the scheme. In direct response to feedback from Year 1 students, who found the scheme very beneficial in enhancing their academic performance and experience, my colleagues were convinced to join the scheme and implement peer-assisted learning in other modules. The power of the student voice ensured the extension of the scheme to cover all Year 1 core modules. Evaluation of the scheme using questionnaires, interviews and focus groups showed the advantages to student participants, resulting in enhanced student engagement, academic performance, learning experience and confidence, while peer leaders strengthened their transferable, leadership and employability skills.

After implementing the successful scheme in the Department of Chemistry, I recognised the potential of peer-assisted learning for a wider impact. Transitioning to higher education is a global issue (Cole, 2017). Collaborative learning, including peer-assisted learning, has been identified as an effective way to address this problem (Van der Meer & Scott, 2009). I disseminated my approach nationally and internationally, through presentations at several conferences and publications, to target relevant audiences. Therefore, I shared my vision and inspired colleagues inside and outside my institution to adopt the scheme so we could achieve a common goal (Martin et al., 2014) and tackle the transition issues.

Transformational leaders not only build relationships via networking but also provide support and guidance to influence change (Raffo & Williams, 2018). Learning from experiences of implementing peer-assisted learning locally and its scope to be tailored to the requirements of other departments, disciplines and institutions, I contributed to scholarly leadership of teaching and learning through authoring two book chapters. These provided educators with step-by-step guidance to design and implement the scheme and showcased my evidence-informed practice (Sedghi, 2019; Sedghi & Washbourn, 2021). The publications led to several requests for advice both inside and outside my home institution on adopting peer-assisted learning.

Peer-assisted learning was adopted by seven departments at my own institution. The departmental academic leads demonstrated the positive impact of the scheme on students' experience by collecting evidence-based data and evaluating the outcomes presented at the University's Learning and Teaching Conference. Again, the power of students' voices was evident as it attracted the University's senior management's attention to the importance of peer-assisted learning. The student panel at the University's Learning and Teaching conference requested that all students across the University should benefit from the scheme, participating as Year 1 students or as leaders if they were students at higher year levels.

Peer mentoring for international students

Since 2012, my Department of Chemistry has accepted students into the second-year undergraduate chemistry courses from Xi'an Jiaotong-Liverpool University, an international university formed in partnership between the University of Liverpool in the UK and Xi'an Jiaotong University in China. Students are taught in English, and the programmes are modelled on Liverpool's programmes but with an introductory first year to prepare them for learning in a UK higher education system. In those subjects where agreements have been reached, Chinese students have the option to complete their final two years of study at the University of Liverpool. Although the Chinese students study in an educational system similar to the UK through their first two years in China, they face the common challenges of international students. Apart from academic issues, entering the second year of study at Liverpool makes integrating home and international students very challenging, as Chinese students are placed alongside an existing cohort of home and sometimes mixed international students in Year 2. Therefore, I decided to explore the challenges, find solutions and prepare the Department of Chemistry to welcome and host the Chinese students.

I was committed to enhancing international students' experience due both to my identity as an international academic and my interest in internationalisation. I secured external and internal funding to develop and implement strategies and activities to enhance home and international students' experience in a multicultural educational environment (Willis & Sedghi, 2014). Based on the lessons I learned from my previous peer-assisted learning project, I ran focus groups of home and international students to bring together the student experiences of internationalisation. I organised staff interviews to learn about the existing provisions, examples of good practice and areas for improvement. As a result, I developed new strategies and introduced new activities, including pre-arrival plans, introductory tutorials, multicultural group work and peer mentoring, to make the student experience enjoyable and applicable to international and UK students.

Findings from the student focus groups indicated home students' interest in contributing to pastoral support to international students. I extended the peer mentoring scheme at the University of Liverpool in order to train new mentors for international students. Peer mentoring is a pastoral system to help the transition of new students into university life. Several chemistry students expressed their interest in mentoring Chinese students. The student mentors and I started communicating with the Chinese students in the summer before their arrival in Liverpool. Chinese students built up a relationship with home students before starting their studies in the UK, which raised their confidence to travel to and live in a foreign country.

The funding allowed me to recruit students as our partners to design a set of curricular and extracurricular activities. This project was another example of strategic leadership without formal managerial or leadership roles. I set up bespoke induction activities for international students on their arrival in order to meet their mentors. I recruited home students as partners to design and deliver the induction sessions for Chinese students. Delivery of pre-arrival and induction activities by trained home students showed 100% international student satisfaction.

I continued my research to develop a set of evidence-informed activities and strategies to enhance home and international students' experiences, including multicultural group activities (Sedghi & Rushworth, 2017). Having a strong purpose of providing inclusive educational environment, a clear set of values and standards, and the importance of the Xi'an Jiaotong-Liverpool and Liverpool partnership, I established a sense of urgency (Kotter, 2007) and influenced a team of colleagues to embed multicultural tutorials and teamwork in their modules.

A set of strategies and activities, curricular and extracurricular, to enhance the integration between home and international students was implemented in the Department of Chemistry. The evaluation of the outcomes showed the effectiveness of providing home and international students with an inclusive teaching and learning environment to enhance their experience and academic performance.

After presenting my evidence-informed practice at conferences and publishing in peer-reviewed journals, I was recognised as an expert in the area of internationalisation. I formally became the Internationalisation Lead in the Department of Chemistry. The new role provided me with a platform to extend activities in this area. As a recognised leader, I was asked to lead a team of staff in the Faculty of Science and Engineering to develop a scheme for collaborative undergraduate projects with our partner university in China. The outcomes of this project showed a significant impact on students' employability and intercultural learning.

My successful work with Chinese students resulted in an invitation to become a member of the 'UK-China Chemistry Special Interest Network', which included seven universities in the UK. I initiated a collaborative educational research project, 'Chinese expectations of education in the UK', between the four universities with similar Chinese partnerships. This collaboration greatly impacted staff at these universities and transformed hundreds of student experiences in the UK and China (Cranwell et al., 2019).

Extending peer-assisted learning

Through these successes, my long-term goal was then to launch a centrally coordinated peer-assisted learning scheme to support academics and student leaders. I recognised, based on Kotter (2008), that as an effective leader I needed to use my influencing power on a continuous basis, and I needed to exert this influence according to the situation at hand. Hence, I exploited my skills of independence, adaptability, open-mindedness and tolerance to build up my network and gain people's trust and confidence in my leadership. I set up short-term goals to go from local to global. I became a member of relevant committees, which was the key turning point in influencing the University's policy to include peer-assisted learning in the staff-student partnership activities. I provided the committees with my evidence-informed practice and successful outcomes. The adoption of peer-assisted learning by all departments/schools as a potential university-wide scheme underwent discussion.

During the pandemic, I worked with students to switch to online peer-assisted learning as a matter of urgency. The lack of interaction between the staff and students during online teaching made the remote delivery of peer-assisted learning more successful than ever. The participation rate was higher than ever, and students asked for more than one weekly session. I took the outcomes to the relevant University committees to acknowledge the importance of the scheme in supporting students during challenging times. The University Education Committee approved a proposal for a centrally coordinated system, and peer-assisted learning was launched in the academic year 2021/22 across three faculties at the University of Liverpool.

As a learning and teaching leader, I kept my long-term goal in mind while focusing on factors I had power over and utilising them to overcome the barriers beyond my control. I developed short-term and long-term goals, directed colleagues to resources, helped to solve their problems, and kept them motivated to achieve our vision. To build on and generate scholarly teaching and learning practice, I disseminated my approach through presentations at several conferences and via publications (Sedghi, 2013). Building professional relationships with like-minded colleagues who had similar transition issues in their institutions allowed me to propagate my practice.

I knew that leaders' credibility and impact were crucial for obtaining the buy-in needed for success (Raffo & Williams, 2018). Hence, I tried to identify challenges through regular feedback, reflecting on potential solutions and improving practice to enhance the student experience. The scheme's evaluation showed that peer-assisted learning enhanced collaborative learning, developed employability skills among the student leaders and was fundamental in ensuring that home and international students adapted to the new academic environments (Sedghi & Lunt, 2015).

Conclusion

Reflecting on my learning and teaching leadership journey, my key recommendation to colleagues committed to enhancing student experience and performance is that you do not need formal authority to become a successful leader (Wergin, 2007). I appreciate universities' investment in various leadership programmes to support employees. However, higher education institutions need to emphasise the importance of leadership for everyone, not only managerial roles. We need a cultural change in higher education to raise the understanding of academics in non-formal leadership roles and be mindful of developing their capacity to become recognised leaders. The two case studies in this book chapter demonstrated my teaching and learning leadership journey, which started from non-formal leadership in peer-assisted learning and extending this to internationalisation.

While leaders may or may not have formal positions of authority, leaders with little decision-making power have more challenges. Having had little power to delegate responsibilities and no team to work with, I had to inspire colleagues to join my team and influence senior management to overcome barriers. I had to juggle between top-down and bottom-up approaches depending on the situation. Although it was highly challenging, the lack of official power made me reach my full leadership potential.

Aspiring leaders need to make informed decisions about their position and where they want to be in the future. They must have a clear vision and purpose, act strategically and set short-term goals. Leadership is not a random act; it needs a clear understanding and strategy in actions. Leaders need to sustain the team by generating trust and confidence. Furthermore, aligning the vision, objectives and goals with the organisational policies and strategies makes everyone's contribution meaningful and increases engagement. Leaders need a clear vision and enhanced communication to influence colleagues.

Resilience is another crucial aspect of becoming a successful leader. Aspiring leaders should not be afraid of unavoidable barriers and mistakes. Instead, they need to learn from experiences to recover from setbacks, adapt to changes and remember that there is always an alternative route to achieve goals. Should you encounter a barrier beyond your control, focus on what you have power over, assess your options to tackle the issues, and find different ways to meet your target, as illustrated in sharing my peer-assisted learning experience earlier in this chapter.

References

Cole, J. S. (2017). Concluding comments about student transition to higher education. *Higher Education: The International Journal of Higher Education Research, 73*(3), 539–551.

Cranwell, P. B., Edwards, M. G., Haxton, K. J., Hyde, J., Page, E. M., Plana, D., Sedghi, G., & Wright, J. S. (2019). Chinese students' expectations versus reality when studying on a UK-China transnational chemistry degree program. *New Directions in the Teaching of Physical Sciences, 14*(1). https://doi.org/10.29311/ndtps.v0i14.3325

Gravett, K., Medland, E., & Winstone, N. E. (2019). Engaging students as co-designers in educational innovation. In S. Lygo-Baker, I. Kinchin, & N. E. Winstone (Eds.), *Engaging student voices in higher education* (pp. 297–313). Palgrave Macmillan.

Hammond, J. A., Bithell, C. P., Jones, L., & Bidgood, P. (2010). A first-year experience of student-directed peer-assisted learning. *Active Learning in Higher Education, 11*(3), 201–212.

Kotter, J. P. (2007). Leading change – Why transformation efforts fail. *Harvard Business Review, 85*(1), 96–103.

Kotter, J. P. (2008). *Power and influence: Beyond formal authority.* Free Press.

Liphadzi, M., Aigbavboa, C. O., & Thwala, W. D. (2017). A theoretical perspective on the difference between leadership and management. *Procedia Engineering, 196*, 478–482.

Martin, J., McCormack, B., Fitzsimons, D., & Spirig, R. (2014). The importance of inspiring a shared vision. *International Practice Development Journal, 4*(2), 1–15.

Nikoloski, K. (2015). Leadership and management: Practice of the art of influence. *Annals of the Constantin Brâncuşi University of Târgu Jiu: Economy Series, 2*(1), 31–39.

Norzailan, Z., Yusof, S. M., & Othman, R. (2016). Developing strategic leadership competencies. *Journal of Advanced Management Science, 4*(1), 66–71.

Raffo, D., & Williams, R. (2018). Evaluating potential transformational leaders: Weighing charisma vs. credibility. *Strategy & Leadership, 46*(6), 28–34.

Sedghi, G. (2013). Peer assisted learning at the department of chemistry for home and international students. *HEA Community Directions, 9*(1), 14–17.

Sedghi, G. (2019). A sustainable peer assisted learning scheme for chemistry undergraduates. In M. K. Seery & C. Mc Donnell (Eds.), *Teaching chemistry in higher education: A festschrift in honour of professor Tina Overton* (pp. 238–248). Creathach Press.

Sedghi, G., & Lunt, T. (2015). The development and implementation of a Peer assisted learning programme at the University of Liverpool. *Learning Development in Higher Education*, Special Edition: Academic Peer Learning. doi:10.47408/jldhe.v0i0.369

Sedghi, G., & Rushworth, L. (2017). The relation between multicultural group work and the integration of home and international students. *New Directions in the Teaching of Physical Sciences, 12*(1).

Sedghi, G., & Washbourn, G. (2021). PAL training and future use in one's career. In A. Strømmen-Bakhtiar, R. Helde, & E. Suzen (Eds.), *Supplemental instruction. Vol, 2 student learning process* (pp. 141–160). Waxmann.

Selznick, P. (1957). *Leadership in administration: A sociological interpretation.* Harper and Row.

van der Meer, J., & Scott, C. (2009). Students' experiences and perceptions of peer assisted study sessions: Towards ongoing improvement. *Journal of Peer Learning, 2*, 3–22.

Wergin, J. F. (Ed.). (2007). *Leadership in place: How academic professionals can find their leadership voice.* Anker.

Willis, I., & Sedghi, G. (2014). Perceptions and experiences of home students involved in welcoming and supporting direct entry 2nd year international students. *Practice and Evidence of Scholarship of Teaching and Learning in Higher Education, 9,* 2–17.

Shallcross, D. E., & Yates, P. C. (2014). *Skills in mathematics and statistics in chemistry and tackling transition.* The Higher Education Academy. www.advance-he.ac.uk/knowledge-hub/skills-mathematics-and-statistics-chemistry-and-tackling-transition

4 Stepping stones towards higher education teaching and learning leadership
A case study on becoming a Deputy Dean

Lucia Zundans-Fraser

Introduction

As with many migrant families in Australia, a good education is seen as an important stepping stone and something that will lead to further opportunities. I was the first in my family to go to university, and it was only well after graduation that I realised how significant this was. At times I felt the weight of expectation while attending university, as being successful and gaining a higher qualification was positioned as an 'intergenerational endeavour' (O'Shea, 2016). This is also significant in my current context as I work at a university that has a very high first-in-family student profile. Like myself, my students are often first-in-family university attendees and need more particular support to ease their transition from secondary school education or a work environment into university study. In this chapter, I will use my role as Deputy Dean as a case study and reflect on how my background and teaching career have been critical stepping stones in my continually evolving teaching and learning leadership approach.

Steps towards learning and teaching leadership

My first full-time teaching job was at a high school (Years 7–12) as a special education expert. Being in the role of special educator meant that I often needed to take on advocacy and mediation roles on behalf of the students in my care. It also required me to engage with a wide variety of stakeholders – students, parents, teachers, school leaders, government departments and funding bodies. The school was also well known for trialling and implementing innovative teaching and learning programmes. It was particularly significant that both the Principal and Deputy Principal valued inclusion and really lived and breathed a collaborative and pastoral approach to education. They truly modelled an inclusive and collaborative leadership approach that I have utilised throughout my career.

After teaching and leading in a range of educational settings (early childhood, primary and secondary), I had the opportunity to move into the higher education sector. I had never imagined doing this as I had a particular view of academia as an austere environment with highly intelligent people and did not believe that I was suited to a career in such an environment – a classic case of imposter syndrome. The term is commonly used to describe feelings, thoughts and perceptions of inferiority and inadequacy with a fear of being exposed as a fraud or unworthy (Cutri et al., 2021; Joshi & Mangette, 2018; Wilkinson, 2020) and where successes are attributed as a fluke, coincidence or due to luck (Hutchins, 2015; Parkman, 2016).

It was a challenge coming from a school setting, where teaching and learning are fundamental to the job, into a higher education environment where it is good to have strong teaching results but teaching and learning are not always positioned as favourably, or as valued, as research. As a result, I have continued to maintain a publishing and research record while in leadership roles even though it has not been a requirement. This has been due to a mix of my strong personal belief about modelling skills and practices to junior academics and a desire to remain eligible for as many future opportunities as possible. My research, scholarship and professional practice have always been in the field of education and focused on teaching and learning. I have led and worked with others through collaborative publications relating to the scholarship of teaching and learning (Zundans-Fraser & Auhl, 2015; Zundans-Fraser & Bain, 2020; Zundans-Fraser & Lancaster, 2012; Zundans-Fraser & Letts, 2019).

Stepping stones in higher education

In 2012, Jarche stated, 'Work is learning and learning is the work'. This is a noteworthy way to look at the work I engage with every day and how it informs my continual growth. It would be fair to say that in my current role as Deputy Dean in the Faculty of Arts and Education, no two days are the same, and I genuinely feel as though I do learn something new each day. My aim is to work in a way that is goal-oriented and collaborative in my own leadership practice. My ongoing enthusiasm for teaching and educational leadership ensures that I continually endeavour to be a quality professional (Black, 2015; Patton, 2021). This passion has been sustained for over 30 years due to the variety of opportunities I have embraced.

For a significant period of my time at Charles Sturt University, I worked as a lecturer who specialised in inclusive education and child development. I then co-led an institution-wide teaching and learning project, later became the Head of the School of Teacher Education and for the past six years have been Deputy Dean in the Faculty of Arts and Education, which has a portfolio emphasis on teaching and learning. My journey to these leadership roles has been mixed. I co-led the teaching and learning project mentioned above with my doctoral supervisor as it was based on many of the key principles I had implemented as part of my own doctoral work, so there was a natural synergy there. A few years later I was encouraged to apply for the Head of School role by numerous colleagues. I viewed this as a positive sign as these were staff that I would need to lead if successful. A strength I brought to the role was my passion for the School, my colleagues, the programmes we offered and our students. I also surrounded myself with the next generation of leaders who had a similar commitment and philosophy regarding the future directions of the School. We adopted an explicitly collaborative approach to leadership, research, and learning and teaching.

With the Deputy Dean role, I was encouraged to apply by senior leaders at the university. To be honest, at the time I thought that perhaps it would be better to spend a few more years in the Head of School role first before taking on a faculty-wide position. After being told I was successful post-interview, I informed the panel of my concerns in taking up the position. I was initially offered the role in an acting capacity with a one-year contract that would allow me to return as Head of School if I found that the faculty position was not a good fit; however, I have been offered two contract renewals since. What has underpinned each of these positions is my prioritisation of teaching and learning in my own practice and, through more recent leadership roles, the opportunity to 'pay it forward' by supporting and mentoring other academics. This has remained important to me because of how formative this type of support has been in my own leadership journey. The positive experience I had during my first teaching appointment highlighted the difference quality leadership and support makes. It significantly impacted my expectations and provided a personal benchmark regarding what was possible in relation to teaching and learning leadership excellence.

Being Deputy Dean

In my role as a teaching and learning leader, I aim to be a facilitator and model, to nurture confidence and healthy self-esteem (a throwback to my first-in-family position), as well as to encourage collaborative practice and teamwork. I have always highly valued a collaborative approach to leadership and through my doctoral studies became particularly interested in the notion of distributed leadership. This approach has been used in some Australian contexts (Carbone et al., 2017; Jones & Harvey, 2017), but it is a challenging approach to embed in long-standing hierarchically structured universities. Being in a leadership position also means that, at times, difficult decisions need to be made where consulting with others is not possible. However, I have been keenly committed to working towards a distributed leadership approach within our faculty to move us away from what may be considered the more traditional model of structural and positional leadership to a shared and collaborative model.

My current role as Deputy Dean in the Faculty of Arts and Education has given me the opportunity to be involved in various teaching and learning initiatives. In this leadership role, I have focused on particular tasks and have chosen to explore three of these in the following section – managing people and networks, dealing with change management and building partnerships.

Role 1: Managing and valuing people and networks

As I have become involved in leadership at a higher level within the university, I have recognised the need to value and manage the people in my new and existing networks. Within the faculty, we have a very small, core leadership team that meets weekly and more frequently when required, which is often the case when we are working on key reports or feedback requests. Each faculty has a Deputy Dean, so about two years ago I started scheduling a fortnightly catch-up meeting for the three of us in this role. We take this time to de-brief, seek advice about any issues that have arisen, and unload.

Within our faculty, I led the establishment of a peer review of teaching process with both formative and summative assessment options. This has now been rolled out, in varying forms, across all three faculties and at institutional level. Staff use this process as an additional method to provide feedback and insight into their teaching. A more formal process is used in instances where staff wish to use peer review as evidence for promotions purposes. I also initiated a faculty-based citation for excellence in teaching and learning. The awards scheme structure mirrors that used for the Australian National Teaching Awards so that there is a natural trajectory for staff to move from internal to national recognition of their teaching excellence.

I have also been committed to supporting and mentoring staff for teaching awards. I am a little conflicted in this space as awards alone do not indicate whether someone is excelling, and writing strong applications is a particular skill; however, awards and recognition are commonly used as a measure or benchmark of success. I recognise that many staff find it a real challenge to put themselves forward for awards, and my faculty encompasses a number of the 'caring professions' (education, social work, human services) where staff are not renowned for highlighting their good work or self-promoting – for them their great work is simply doing their job.

Role 2: Dealing with change management

Change management has been central to my various leadership roles. I was Head of School at a time when all Schools across the university moved to a new administrative support model, the Common Support Model (CSM), and we shifted to a three-faculty structure. Post-implementation, I continued to work on changes to the CSM, leading a university-wide working group, and also took a leadership role among the Heads of School in the Faculty of Arts and Education as we navigated a newly implemented Academic Workload Manager (AWM) system and workload issues. I continued my advocacy in this space as I moved into the Deputy Dean role. Being the conduit between university executive management and staff on the ground as we navigated the implementation of the CSM was a challenge. It was difficult when staff had been assured of certain levels of support that did not eventuate. This meant needing to lead the working group in a different way, where we pivoted to a focus on how to most strategically use the resources we had rather than what had originally been anticipated. Although there were benefits to having a centralised administrative model, there were significant operational challenges. An underlying principle of the model was that the same process could work in all situations and in all faculties in the same manner when in practice that just was not the case.

Role 3: Building partnerships

In both the Head of School and Deputy Dean roles, I have been responsible for building strategic teaching and learning partnerships within, and outside of, the institution. I have also been centrally involved in cross-faculty working groups looking at governance in learning and teaching as well as student academic integrity. The Deputy Dean role has required me to work closely with other leaders within our faculty to coordinate responses to the Higher Education Standards (HES) framework and account for the various ways our teaching and learning practice meets these standards. I then work with cross-faculty colleagues to discuss effective processes and practices that have been put in place and consider whether any should be implemented institution-wide.

I meet with the six Heads of School (HoS) in our faculty fortnightly, on an individual basis, to discuss issues that are pertinent to them in relation to their School and to also 'check in' regarding particular faculty and institutional priorities at the time. Manning and Curtis (2015) note various conditions that lead to more effective change and positive work environments including a shared vision, shared culture, internal communications, consideration and trust, maintenance and government, and participation and shared leadership. As far as possible, I have tried to implement these types of conditions in my environment and leadership practice. As mentioned earlier, I am very taken by the notion of distributed leadership that incorporates some of the conditions noted by Manning and Curtis, such as shared leadership and vision, although the typically hierarchical nature of a university is not really conducive to this. However, within the smaller teams I lead daily we definitely take more of a shared leadership approach. An outsider joining any of our meetings would have a difficult time determining who is the most senior positionally based on our interactions and working style. By maintaining regular contact with those

I supervise, we are able to build an environment and culture of trust. This is important to do so that my direct reportees feel comfortable sharing both the positive and challenging things that occur so we can jointly problem-solve when necessary.

The affordances of being a Deputy Dean

The irony is that as more senior leadership opportunities have arisen, teaching students, which was my main attractor to tertiary education in the first place, has become a distant memory. Nearly a decade ago, I led an all-institution teaching and learning project that looked at the student lifecycle. This was an incredible experience that gave me the opportunity to work with staff at all levels of the university, from the Vice-Chancellor down, across all faculties and divisions. The initial 'proof of concept' work had been undertaken in my own faculty with purposeful, intensive working sessions with academics and educational designers focused on course design and development. This same approach was then implemented at scale across all three faculties. The project eventually petered out as systems were not quite there to support the work, and without commitment and leadership at executive level, the project became subsumed into a division with bits and pieces 'cherry-picked' for continuation.

My current role has meant a bit more of a pivot back to students and one of the areas I have oversight of is academic misconduct and integrity. I work with a committed team of academics and professional staff who have really tried to take a proactive and educative approach with students and incorporate best practice in a highly sensitive space (Bretag, 2019; Rundle et al., 2020).

Final thoughts

My advice for future leaders would be to seize opportunities that present themselves and do not be afraid to put yourself forward for things. Committee representation is often a good starting point. At my institution there are cycles of membership on key committees and regular call outs for nominations. This does not mean saying 'yes' to everything but to think about a trajectory of representation that leads to committees that have cross-institutional representation where you can get yourself 'known' and provide a voice. Taking an active role on committees exposes you to academic memo writing, how to succinctly put your point across, and an understanding of the governance processes within the institution.

Once you are working in the higher education context, people are unaware of what leadership experiences you have previously had and pivot to a positional focus as an identifier. It is important to advocate in various spaces where your expertise can be recognised and be seen as more than a position.

During my time in the School of Teacher Education, I sat on every committee in operation – research, ethics, staffing, assessment, school board. Since moving into higher leadership roles, I have served on various faculty and university committees. In all cases, I have needed to be well aware of governance and compliance requirements as well as the general sentiment of other staff on key issues so that I can accurately represent views beyond my own. I am a national assessor for *Australian Awards for University Teaching* (AAUT) citations. This has given me the opportunity to work with academics across various Australian institutions who are equally passionate about teaching and learning but are typically outside of my own discipline. I have served on multiple teacher education course accreditation panels where I have had the opportunity to engage with other academics and school leaders. I have also undertaken assessment benchmarking with other higher education institutions in my areas of expertise of special/inclusive education and child development. This broad range of educational and staff development activity ensures the currency of my own practice and enables my connections to the field to inform my teaching and leadership.

The events that have shaped my teaching and learning journey included here are not exhaustive, and there are many others that could have been included; however, these represent key turning points or considerations in my career. My leadership journey has been punctuated by moments of uncertainty, success, contradictions and unexpected events – all of which add to my identity and experience as a leader. This identity will continue to evolve over my lifetime and it has been an absolute pleasure to develop and learn over the decades through my interactions with students and colleagues.

References

Black, S. A. (2015). Qualities of effective leadership in higher education. *Open Journal of Leadership, 4*, 54–66. doi:10.4236/ojl.2015.42006

Bretag, T. (2019). From 'perplexities of plagiarism' to 'building cultures of integrity': A reflection on fifteen years of academic integrity research, 2003–2018. *HERDSA Review of Higher Education, 6*, 5–35.

Carbone, A., Evans, J., Ross, B., Drew, S., Phelan, L., Lindsay, K., Cottman, C., Stoney, S., & Ye, J. (2017). Assessing distributed leadership for learning and teaching quality: A multi-institutional study. *Journal of Higher Education Policy and Management, 39*(2), 183–196. doi:10.1080/1360080X.2017.1276629

Cutri, J., Abraham, A., Karlina, Y., Patel, S. V., Moharami, M., Zeng, S., Manzari, E., & Pretorius, L. (2021). Academic integrity at doctoral level: The influence of the imposter phenomenon and cultural differences on academic writing. *International Journal of Educational Integrity, 17*(8). doi:10.1007/s40979-021-00074-w

Hutchins, H. M. (2015). Outing the imposter: A study exploring imposter phenomenon among higher education faculty. *New Horizons in Adult Education & Human Resource Development, 27*(2), 3–12.

Jarche, H. (2012, June 17). *Work is learning and learning is the work*. Blog posting. https://jarche.com/2012/06/work-is-learning-and-learning-is-the-work/

Jones, S., & Harvey, M. (2017). A distributed leadership change process model for higher education. *Journal of Higher Education Policy and Management, 39*(2), 126–139. doi:10.1080/1360080X.2017.1276661

Joshi, A., & Mangette, H. (2018). Unmasking of impostor syndrome. *Journal of Research, Assessment, and Practice in Higher Education, 3*(1), 1–8.

Manning, G., & Curtis, K. (2015). *The art of leadership* (5th ed.). McGraw-Hill Education.

O'Shea, S. (2016). First-in-family learners and higher education: Negotiating the 'silences' of university transition and participation. *HERDSA Review of Higher Education, 3*, 5–23.

Parkman, A. (2016). The imposter phenomenon in higher education: Incidence and impact. *Journal of Higher Education Theory and Practice, 16*(1), 51–60.

Patton, W. (2021). The many faces of leadership: Leading people and change in Australian higher education. *Journal of Educational Administration and History, 53*(2), 121–131. doi:10.1080/00220620.2020.1793740

Rundle, K., Curtis, G., & Clare, J. (2020). Why students choose not to cheat. In T. Bretag (Ed.), *A research agenda for academic integrity* (pp. 100–111). Edward Elgar Publishing.

Wilkinson, C. (2020). Imposter syndrome and the accidental academic: An autoethnographic account. *International Journal for Academic Development, 25*(4), 363–374. doi:10.1080/1360144X.2020.1762087

Zundans-Fraser, L., & Auhl, G. (2015). A theory-driven approach to course design in inclusive education. *Australian Journal of Teacher Education, 41*(3), 140–157.

Zundans-Fraser, L., & Bain, A. (2020). Making a difference to the student experience through purposeful course design. *Australian Journal of Teacher Education, 45*(8), 58–74. doi:10.14221/ajte.2020v45n8.4

Zundans-Fraser, L., & Lancaster, J. (2012). Enhancing the inclusive self-efficacy of pre-service teachers through embedded course design. *Education Research International, 2012*. www.hindawi.com/journals/edu/2012/581352/

Zundans-Fraser, L., & Letts, W. (2019). School-university partnerships: Strengthening professional experience relationships. *Transform – The Journal of Engaged Scholarship, 4*, 50–52.

5 Opportunities and barriers to leadership in student support services

A case study of inclusive assessment

Silvia Colaiacomo and Tom Sharp

Introduction and context

This case study articulates an 'alternative' leadership trajectory based on the collaboration and cross-pollination of student support services, student-led projects and academic developers. The focus is on the development of leadership in learning and teaching in non-academic roles and the value of context sensitivity and bottom-up approaches to inform policy and institutional strategies. The case study is co-authored by an academic developer who is also a lecturer in higher education (SC) and a student support manager (TS) and relates to an inclusive assessment project initiated in 2019, before both authors moved to different roles and universities. The main narrative will be presented in the first person from the perspective of TS. SC's role in the case study was that of a mentor, as she provided the theoretical framework, language and tools for TS' trajectory to shape. Whilst her role in the activities presented in the case study is mostly 'invisible', the reflection on the impact of the work outlined in the chapter could only come to light through conversations and collaborations between the two authors. With this chapter, we propose a model of informal mentorship that values personal and professional growth regardless of official paths of career promotion or institutional hierarchies.

We define leadership as the ability to take initiatives and make decisions in contexts beyond the constraints or limitations of set institutional frameworks (Fairholm & Fairholm, 2000). For us, leadership is the act of collaboration, of seeking opportunities for colleagues to grow, from the perspective of benefitting the students, their independence and critical engagement with their studies. Hence, leadership is about designing and taking the lead on innovative projects, identifying areas for structural improvement and piloting close collaborations between different areas of the university, including student-led initiatives. This leadership approach rooted in collaborative work can be defined as 'invisible'. Invisible leadership (Sorenson & Hickman, 2002) emerges when people become advocates and embodiments of the common purpose, in this case students' capabilities to perform at their best (Terzi, 2007), and live a positive university experience, whilst not seeking recognition through mechanisms of self-promotion and visibility.

This case study is contextualised within the backdrop of changes to management and funding that have affected higher education in the UK and largely reshaped the role and perception of universities as service providers for students, conceptualised as customers (Woodall et al., 2014). Much has been researched and written about workload, working conditions and their relationship to burnout, particularly in student support services (Brewer & Clippard, 2002; Gibbs, 2013; Macdonald et al., 2018; Randle & Zainuddin, 2020). Student support staff often act as a first point of contact for students in relation to a number of needs and scenarios, from attainment, to finances, to well-being. The role of student support services may be conceptualised as remedial (Yolak et al., 2019) or, in contrast, fundamental to student development associated with transferable skills, confidence and employability (Andrew & Russell, 2012).

TS: leadership trajectory

I (TS) was recruited into higher education to support students with disabilities after four years of experience in further education. The university required a disability practitioner who would interpret and apply the obligations of the Special Educational Needs and Disabilities Act (2001). The most urgent need was the facilitation of one-to-one support mechanisms (recruitment and allocation of support workers to disabled students), for academic purposes. The service coordinator campaigned for policy, and as an assistant, I took forward the policies into practice. My role became more specialist as a disability practitioner, advising on accommodation and advocating for access across the university estate. Mediation, practical interventions, liaison and communication with students on a daily basis, all forged the vitality of the role. The second phase of my tenure (2007–13) witnessed the increased demand for autism support alongside provision for students with disabilities. I led supervision of academic support teams, including autism mentoring, and the provision and dissemination of good practice via learning support plans. The third phase of my employment followed another restructure and can be dated from my appointment as Disability Team Lead (2013–21) as part of an enlarged management structure. Formal recognition of my supervision duties and leadership role in learning and teaching specialism was supported by the recruitment of additional specialist staff.

My greatest achievement as a disability practitioner and learning and teaching specialist in the university where the case study is based, was the willingness to recruit and lead teams of support staff, to create innovative support systems in which both staff and students felt valued and rewarded. The university failed to provide secure working contracts for the majority of student facing staff, and yet many staff demonstrated commitment and remained in service on rolling contracts. Within my permanent staff team, there was great continuity, with several team members having over 10 years of experience. Beyond my immediate line management practice, we recruited specialist staff to lead on autism project activities, expanding the remit of the service. As a result of a willingness to design and supervise activities that enhance the student experience, we evolved a culture of social support networks. The disability office was conceived in order to ensure the institution met statutory duties, but in practice, we recruited disabled students into disability practitioner roles and this led to a change in culture (Kezar & Eckel, 2002) in learning and teaching within the disability team, and across the university.

The problem: institutional culture and challenges to student support

The work of the disability office existed within an environment that had structural challenges. Firstly, the data storage systems used to monitor students' academic journey were not integrated and resulted in students' data being duplicated up to four times. The implementation of data storage systems was the responsibility of all staff, disability specialists and administrators. It was the case that this created a massive increase in staff time dedicated to keeping digital storage systems updated and accurate (Gloet & Berrell, 2003). This, inevitably, meant that less time was available to meet with students with disabilities, and develop and implement support strategies and individualised learning and teaching plans.

The second challenge was that, at the time of the case study, the university enforced a blanket freeze on recruitment to attempt to overcome financial difficulties, which meant recruitment increasingly required the approval of senior staff. Given that support staff contracts were not permanent, and not highly remunerative, it then became more difficult to retain specialised staff. Hence, students were seeking support in ever-increasing numbers, and particularly for issues relating to wellbeing, that required both recruitment and specialisation of key roles. On the other hand, the university strategy was moving in the opposite direction by seeking to reduce costs via removing appointments and training opportunities for specialised staff.

Institutional challenges

For each disabled student who registers for support a learning support plan is created which is shared with the academic teams. And yet, at the time of the case study, there was minimal dialogue between academic teams and disability practitioners regarding the implementation of the plan. Engagement with academic staff, unfortunately, usually occurred only in response to crisis situations where a disabled student had not met the requirements of the academic programme, or where the student's particular, specific disability requirements were set outside the standard provision of the institution. In these situations, academic staff commonly delegated the liaison and negotiation required to departmental student support coordinators. Academic staff would sometimes be drawn into a discussion regarding the adjustment of assessment practices, but in my experience, academic teams did not expect disability practitioners to influence teaching and learning, despite these teams being highly knowledgeable in the field. As such, successful disabled students would be those who could readily absorb the requirements of the academic course with minor adjustments (such as re-timetabling of assessments). The students who did not readily adapt to academic systems were those most likely to require the intervention of a disability practitioner.

The inclusive assessment project

Within the context outlined above, in 2018/19 we (SC and TS) worked together on an inclusive assessment project. The project aimed to raise awareness of assessment design that could unintentionally result in additional difficulties for diverse student cohorts; for example, neurodiverse students may differently interpret and approach a task, which in turn may lead to failure (Nieminen, 2022). The project aimed to develop a common language of assessment instructions and a shared framework that would guide academic staff when designing assignments which could be successfully completed by a diverse student population. Barriers to assessment can be identified in a lack of, or poor, assessment literacy (Taylor, 2009); taken-for-granted assumptions about how to complete a task against a set of given criteria are not necessarily obvious to students unless the format has been thoroughly explained in advance. For example, a neurodivergent student could stall during assessment where the literal reading of a question presents ambiguity. Against the institutional backdrop outlined in the previous sections of this chapter, the leading of the project was even more complex and challenging, as it was not supported by a broader ethos of staff development and overall availability of resources.

Our approach to the problem

The aim of our initiative was to create a local hub for assessment innovation, underpinned by the principles of universal design (Rose, 2000) and informed by the expertise of academics working in specific disciplines, educationalists and digital learning experts, professional services, student support and disability services, and student representatives. The main driver for assessment-related projects at our institution was a response to national student satisfaction metrics; these metrics, as they influenced the ranking of universities, provided us with an excellent opportunity to invite colleagues from student support teams and student representatives to join a shared conversation on learning and teaching priorities.

We set up training for academics on assessment design and literacy by inviting experts in the sector from other institutions as well as student representatives. We also engaged in conversation with our exam office to develop a better understanding of the practical context of assessment, as the arrangements made by the exam office in terms of logistics, timetabling, location, number of students gathered in the same venue, etc. inevitably shaped assessment conditions and affected performance.

The discussion and understanding of the local context between the authors and other staff were crucial to generate awareness of teams' capabilities, potential and output that culminated in the initiative taken with the inclusive assessment project. In a way, the numerous barriers we faced served as an opportunity to reflect on what invisible leadership is, and how it operates and can influence colleagues despite not being explicitly invested with a position of power.

The project, which stalled due to change in staff and later the COVID-19 pandemic, brought student support services to the core of the discussion about what constitutes leadership in learning and teaching, not as a remedial service, but as a key player in shaping curriculum, assessment and pedagogy. We were able to pilot a shared leadership approach (Pearce et al., 2008) that proved to be both innovative and effective. As well as invisible leadership, both in terms of providing unintrusive support and promoting the 'common good' over individual promotional paths, the relationships established in the project informed the collaboration between colleagues regardless of their official title within the institutional hierarchy. The inclusive assessment project triggered a reflection on the value of collaboration across teams and an alternative conceptualisation of leadership in learning and teaching in terms of leading change through cooperation and bottom-up initiatives (Fraser et al., 2006). The reflection led to a new consideration of student support roles and their broader impact across university life and learning and teaching strategies.

Lessons learned

Our case study highlighted a structural lack of communication and reflection regarding roles, responsibilities and evolution of services between senior managers and those who work directly with students as well as a lack of critical engagement with student input and feedback. As communication stalls, opportunities to work in synergy with other central areas of the university are affected. The expertise and first-hand experiences of staff can be key not only to inform individual interventions but also to shape policy and curriculum choices as well as approaches to assessment, the use of technology and a holistic view of the student experience. To move towards a more comprehensive approach to student support in learning and teaching means to value the experience and expertise of colleagues working in different areas of the university and equally to bring students to the core of the discussion.

Therefore, the approach we used with the inclusive assessment project provided a good example of shared and invisible leadership, since the focus on expertise rather than official roles generated a disruptive pattern in the usual running of the institution in relation to assessment design and delivery. We advocated for an approach to higher education that builds upon the lived experience of its community and identifies examples of learning and teaching leadership beyond the constraints of set managerial and/or senior academic roles. Such an approach also provided opportunities for academic and professional development to colleagues in support roles through informal mentorship, so that they could build and articulate a discourse of teaching and learning leadership and a whole-rounded awareness of their impact and influence at institutional level.

A humanist approach to student support and staff management (Spitzeck, 2011) implies juggling the contradictory reality of data outcomes and conflicting priorities. To create the conditions for students to thrive and be challenged and to make the most of our staff expertise, motivation and abilities, we need to invite all parties to join conversations, cyclical work reviews and to set up collaborative projects where different inputs are considered and equally valued. At the same time, we need to support the development of self-awareness and agency in colleagues who are generally not included in leadership discourses, by inviting them to engage with collaborative projects through which they can articulate their teaching and learning leadership approach. We will not be able to create a cohesive community of colleagues and students working together unless we conceptualise teaching and learning leadership as shared and multi-layered, and we strengthen trust, respect and an open approach to problem-solving that welcomes different perspectives.

Conclusions

Through examining the case study of the inclusive assessment project, with its challenges of data management and increasing student demand, we propose that much can be achieved by engaging senior managers, academics, professional services and students in collaborative projects through shared leadership (Pearce et al., 2008) and invisible leadership (Hickman, 2004) in teaching and learning. To value intergenerational and diverse communities of colleagues and students can unlock possibilities for bottom-up change, and innovative and empowering practice. By doing so, leadership in teaching and learning becomes an approach to innovation and change rather than the fulfilment of a static professional position description. Also, we want to stress that leadership in teaching and learning is silently enacted in areas of professional and support services that can be overlooked by official policy and strategic consultations. To make these areas more central to policy discussion, we need to strengthen collaborative projects where expertise can be showcased, and outcomes closely linked to improving student and staff experiences can be celebrated. This is a form of leadership in action that results in highly effective impact in terms of student experience and attainment and whose success is paradoxically measured by the extent of its silent, invisible leadership and support to other areas of the university, such as academics and academic developers. By providing a voice and developing a shared language to this leadership through informal mentorship, communication between colleagues working in different areas, and co-leading projects, we aim to reshape educational provision with a holistic perspective. Collaborative projects that bring together and value different forms of expertise and experience can massively contribute to creating a broader awareness of the interplay of teaching and learning with support roles that are traditionally conceptualised as remedial.

References

Andrew, G., & Russell, M. (2012). Employability skills development: Strategy, evaluation and impact. *Higher Education, Skills and Work-Based Learning, 2*(1), 33–44. https://doi.org/10.1108/20423891211197721

Brewer, F. W., & Clippard, L. F. (2002). Burnout and job satisfaction among student support services personnel. *Human Resources Development Quarterly, 13*(2), 169–186. https://doi.org/10.1002/hrdq.1022

Fairholm, M. R., & Fairholm, G. (2000). Leadership amid the constraints of trust. *Leadership & Organization Development Journal, 21*(2), 102–109. https://doi.org/10.1108/01437730010318192

Fraser, E. D. G., Dougill, A. J., Mabee, W. E., Reed, M., & McAlpine, P. (2006). Bottom up and top down: Analysis of participatory processes for sustainability indicator identification as a pathway to community empowerment and sustainable environmental management. *Journal of Environmental Management, 78*(2), 114–127. https://doi.org/10.1016/j.jenvman.2005.04.009

Gibbs, E. (2013). Equal but different: The marketisation of disability support. *Overland* (212), 36–43. https://search.informit.org/doi/10.3316/ielapa.201223856

Gloet, M., & Berrell, M. (2003). The dual paradigm nature of knowledge management: Implications for achieving quality outcomes in human resource management. *Journal of Knowledge Management, 7*(1), 78–89. https://doi.org/10.1108/13673270310463635

Gunn, A. (2018). Metrics and methodologies for measuring teaching quality in higher education: Developing the teaching excellence framework (TEF). *Educational Review*, *70*(2), 129–148. doi:10.1080/00131911.2017.1410106

Joseph, N. (2020). Marketising disability services: A love-hate relationship in a neoliberal world. *Social Work & Policy Studies: Social Justice, Practice and Theory*, *2*(2), Student Edition. https://openjournals.library.sydney.edu.au/SWPS/article/view/14059

Macdonald, F., Bentham, E., & Malone, J. (2018). Wage theft, underpayment and unpaid work in marketised social care. *The Economic and Labour Relations Review*, *29*(1), 80–96. doi:10.1177/1035304618758252

Nieminen, J. H. (2022). Assessment for inclusion: Rethinking inclusive assessment in higher education. *Teaching in Higher Education*. doi:10.1080/13562517.2021.2021395

Pearce, C. L., Conger, J. A., & Locke, E. A. (2008). Shared leadership theory. *The Leadership Quarterly*, *19*(5), 622–628. https://doi.org/10.1016/j.leaqua.2008.07.005.

Randle, M., & Zainuddin, N. (2020). Value creation and destruction in the marketisation of human services. *Journal of Services Marketing*. https://doi.org/10.1108/JSM-10-2019-0424

Rose, D. (2000). Universal design for learning. *Journal of Special Education Technology*, *15*(3), 45–49. doi:10.1177/016264340001500307

Sorenson, G., & Hickman, G. R. (2002). Invisible leadership: Acting on behalf of a common purpose. In C. Cherrey & R. Matusak (Eds.), *Building leadership bridges* (pp. 7–24). James MacGregor Academy of Leadership.

Spitzeck, H. (2011). An integrated model of humanistic management. *Journal of Business Ethics*, *99*, 51–62. https://doi.org/10.1007/s10551-011-0748-6

Taylor, L. (2009). Developing assessment literacy. *Annual Review of Applied Linguistics*, *29*, 21–36. doi:10.1017/S0267190509090035

Terzi, L. (2007). Capability and educational equality: The just distribution of resources to students with disabilities and special educational needs. *Journal of Philosophy of Education*, *41*(4), 757–773.

Woodall, T., Hiller, A., & Resnick, R. (2014). Making sense of higher education: Students as consumers and the value of the university experience. *Studies in Higher Education*, *39*(1), 48–67. doi:10.1080/03075079.2011.648373

Yolak, B. B., Kiziltepe, Z., & Seggie, F. N. (2019). The contribution of remedial courses on the academic and social lives of secondary school students. *Journal of Education*, *199*(1), 24–34. doi:10.1177/0022057419836434

6 Be(com)ing an academic leader

A case study on a collaborative partnership for external peer review

Josephine Lang

Entering the university sector

My path to teaching and learning leadership in universities did not start in January of 2000 with my first position as a tutor, while commencing my part-time PhD studies. Rather, I brought along with me over a decade of my lived experiences as secondary school teacher, curriculum leader, zoo education practitioner, curriculum policy officer in government, president of two professional associations and influencer of educational policies. With my backstory as a successful secondary school teacher undertaking diverse roles of learning and teaching leadership, I did not expect my transition into higher education would be challenging; teaching is teaching, after all – or so I naively thought. Engaging in levels of phronesis, I had to disrupt my early gestalt (Korthagen et al., 2001) to build new knowledge and practice that addressed novel complexities in the different workplace contexts I found myself in. While my early gestalt about teaching pre-service teachers held elements of truth for me, it did not portray the complexity of the work of the teacher educator or my journey of becoming a leader for teaching and learning in the higher education sector. The notion of transitions from (teaching) practitioner to academic, with a view towards academic leadership is not peculiar to me, and the challenges that arise in professional identity and practice in making such transitions are common place (e.g. Dickinson et al., 2020; Zeichner, 2005).

In this chapter, I will explore my professional trajectory of teaching and learning leadership in higher education through one narrative from my lived experience 'as a way to understand experience and a way to study experience' (Clandinin, 2013, p. 15). Using a narrative inquiry approach, this case study represents an example of a rich opportunity in my career and provides insights into what I have learned about teaching and learning leadership in higher education.

DOI: 10.4324/9781003360018-8

A conceptual framework for leadership analysis

Leadership for teaching and learning is an evolving (Marshall et al., 2011; Mason & de la Harpe, 2020) and contested (Middlehurst, 2008; Youngs, 2017) field. However, while many research studies on leadership look at qualities the academic leader should possess (Bryman, 2007) or the leadership styles they should engage with (Legood et al., 2021), Juntrasook (2014) provides an alternative way to make meaning of academic leadership for teaching and learning that he arrived at in his study of extended narratives of academic leaders. He generates four categories of meaning about leadership in academia:

- *Leadership as position* – undertaking a formal leadership role within the academy;
- *Leadership as performance* – focuses on performance as a leader that can be audited and measured;
- *Leadership as practice* – the professional practice of academic leaders in their everyday contexts; focuses on the interactions with others and often associated with the movement of distributed leadership;
- *Leadership as professional role model* – associated with being a leader that acts as role model, mentoring, coaching and inspiring others.

Juntrasook (2014) identifies leadership as position and leadership as performance as categories that can be observed or measured. For their observable and measurable qualities, Juntrasook (2014) suggests that these categories are easier to define. Although I suppose whether we measure what is important in leadership may be up for debate, as often we measure what is easy to quantify. In contrast, Juntrasook (2014) argues the latter two leadership categories are more ambiguous, particularly as they are socially constructed and open to multiple interpretations. Juntrasook's categories are a useful framework for me to reflect on and analyse my own be(com)ing leadership trajectory through my case study on the Network of Associate Deans of Learning And Teaching in the discipline of Education (NADLATE) Chair.

NADLATE Chair: developing a collaborative and dialogic external peer review process

Context

In the Australian university regulatory context, Tertiary Education Quality and Standards Agency (TEQSA)[1] significantly revised the Higher Education Standards Framework (Threshold Standards) in 2015 from its inaugural 2011 version. The Higher Education Standards Framework represents key regulatory requirements for Australian higher education providers to ensure the quality of student experience across the student lifecycle.

One key area of change was associated within Domain 5, particularly in 5.3 *Monitoring, Review and Improvement*, where regular external referencing or other benchmarking activities are now an expectation in periodic comprehensive accredited course reviews. In some respects, this policy change to increase the profile of external peer review of curriculum may be seen as TEQSA, a government agency, wanting to increase accountability of higher education providers to improve the quality of learning; and this is likely to be at least partially true. Yet, such a perception of TEQSA's reform agenda ensures that the power resides with the regulatory agency and that they determine what and how things are measured to frame quality teaching and learning outputs. At the time of this policy change, I was working in academic leadership roles within my faculty (e.g. Associate Dean of Teaching and Learning) as well as across Australia's network of academic leaders within education faculties (e.g. NADLATE Chair – Network of Associate Deans of Learning And Teaching in the discipline of Education, a network of the Australian Council of Deans of Education, ACDE).

In reacting to the policy change, I decided to re-frame how I looked at the *problem* of TEQSA's emphasis on external peer review and benchmarking of curriculum. Rather than a threat, I re-framed this as an *opportunity* for NADLATE to 'tak[e] charge of our own accountability' (Lucas, 2000, p. 1) to collaborate and define our own measures and protocols to ensure academic quality through co-designing our own rigorous quality assurance model for initial teacher education programmes in Australia. While other jurisdictions may have well-established processes for such external referencing and benchmarking activities (e.g. in the UK, regulation and guidance by the Quality Assurance Agency (QAA), and the Higher Education Academy (HEA) (now Advance HE) Handbook for External Examiners, 2012); in Australia, it is still a relatively new concept and practice. Hence, for me, TEQSA's reform in this area raises the issue of an 'institutional gap' in professional knowledge and practice of external peer review and benchmarking within the Australian initial teacher education context. In discussion with the NADLATE Steering Group about the focus of the year's work, I took on leading the external peer review project in 2018 as the NADLATE Chair. Aligned with my re-framing of the TEQSA policy change, I shaped the project to focus on generating a productive learning community, which would take the opportunity to co-design a model of external peer review that transformed our practices in and across education faculties and inform future programme design. Such an approach to focus on learning to lead change in higher education for transformative outcomes has also been argued by others (e.g. Angelo, 2000).

The NADLATE project was to design and trial a process of external peer review of assessment in initial teacher education programmes. After a call for expressions of interest across NADLATE's national membership of about 40 education faculties, six Australian universities participated in the pilot, which involved 29 academic and professional staff, who nominated undergraduate or postgraduate programmes and nine relevant assessment tasks for the purposes of benchmarking and external peer review. As we had not worked together on a project previously, I created time for the team to share our aspirations for the project, which informed our focus, the co-design of protocols, and development of adapted tools for the work of external curriculum peer review. On reflection, this collaborative approach taps into the theories of action discussed by Gallos and Bolman and emphasises the efficacy of a model of action theory reliant on 'high advocacy coupled with high inquiry' (Gallos & Bolman, 2021, p. 44) and is based on the work of organisational theorists Chris Argyris and Donald Schön. In framing the project as a collaborative partnership to explore the problem (i.e. how to develop a process for external peer review and benchmarking of programmes that meet the revised policy standards governing higher education providers), as the lead, I shaped the cultural tone for the way we learned and worked together. It was a collaborative generation of our hopes and ways of working towards our common goal of designing a dialogic, purposeful and professional learning approach to external peer review of curriculum. To make the work of external peer review meaningful and manageable, we decided to create small teams of two or three institutions to work on similar subjects and associated assessment. This decision of matching teams across expertise, also ensured the teacher educator curriculum discipline expertise required for the external peer review was in place.

The project comprised of four phases:

- *Preliminary* – identification of programme, subject, assessment task for external peer review;
- *Establishing* – through a collaborative inquiry partnership approach identify the focus and develop partner protocols, tools, resource sharing and small team creation (pairs or triads);
- *Peer Review* – initial individual assessment of the curriculum > intra-institution moderation among the institution's members for the external peer review > sharing of findings with partnering institution(s) using draft Review Reports to stimulate discussion and clarify matters;
- *Sharing* – finalisation of Review Reports; project findings about the process across the whole team; sharing with rest of NADLATE and ACDE members at the ACDE national forum.

In the Peer Review phase, as individuals we used the curriculum review tool that we co-developed as a whole group in the Establishing phase. We used the tool to peer review the partnering institution(s)' assessment task design and guidance, samples of preservice teacher assignment artefacts and marking. Then each institutional team moderated their individual external peer review assessments to determine an institutional report of the external peer review. These moderated institutional reports were used to stimulate discussion through the sharing of external peer review report protocol with the partnering institution(s) and provided the impetus to clarify assumptions, queries or misunderstandings through the debriefing session of the peer review and benchmarking process.

Impact of the peer review of assessment in initial teacher education project

To capture and represent our professional learning in designing and piloting the external peer review and benchmarking process, I asked the project members to reflect on their experience to inform any future NADLATE revision of this process and its use. These reflections on what we learned from undertaking the project were presented at the national ACDE forum in late 2018. According to the project team, the best aspects included the cross-institutional opportunity:

- to work in teams;
- to share programme structures and learn from curriculum work and its design;
- for deepening engagement and insights of accreditation requirements;
- to have professional conversations to clarify, debate and refine our work as teacher educators;
- to work with student work samples to enable authentic and rich conversations about assessment within current teacher education and policy debates;
- to reflect on own institutional practices while opening a space for our partners to contribute new ways of thinking about our practices.

Alternatively, reflection on areas for improvement seemed to focus on technical issues associated with a new process that is in pilot mode:

- *clarity on roles and responsibilities* – participating in the project on top of already overstretched workloads sometimes meant roles/responsibilities were not always fully understood by individuals;
- *peer review portal* – the purpose-built portal was still in the early stages of development and was abandoned after it consistently failed during the project;
- *context is important* – to understand curriculum and assessment design, which facilitates a purposeful peer review;
- *protect privacy of student data* – shared as assessment samples for peer review.

54 *Josephine Lang*

Finally, recommendations included strategies such as:

- finding an appropriate way to share the relevant institutional data with fit-for-purpose technology;
- continued use of the team and dialogic approach used in the pilot that enabled authentic professional learning for the Associate Deans Teaching and Learning (ADTLs);
- introduce subject orientation prior to peer review in each pair or triad;
- reinforce the activity purpose for each phase of the external peer review process;
- streamline the Peer Review Reports.

These reflections add further empirical evidence to themes explored by Lucas and her colleague Angelo (Lucas, 2000) about the role that collaborative learning communities can achieve to provide a deeper and purposeful academic change in higher education. On reflection, I can see that deeply interweaving the professional learning element into the NADLATE project ensured that we could identify problems as we engaged in academic change and either resolve them or think about future strategies for improvement.

Analysis of the leadership approach and my learning

The NADLATE Chair is an honorary position elected by ADTL peers in the Steering Group (about a dozen ADTLs) that represents all states and territories of Australia from the full Network.[2]

Using Juntrasook's (2014) leadership categories to analyse my lived experience in be(com)ing the academic leader in the context of the NADLATE Chair afforded me to see the nature of teaching and learning leadership in higher education. I chose this example because it provided a boundary to reflect on an aspect of my academic leadership over time. As Middlehurst (2008) has argued, context is significant in theory, practice and learning of academic leadership as context influences the ways leaders respond, act and transfer theory into practice.

Through the analysis, represented in Table 6.1, I realise the interactions between the meanings of academic leadership categories. This is also acknowledged by Juntrasook: 'these four meanings of leadership [categories] were overlapping but distinguishable, employing distinctive tropes, metaphors and statements' (2014, p. 22).

What I learned from this reflective analysis is that teaching and learning leadership is complex and dynamic, and draws on different knowledge, skills and mindsets with each situation and context of the leadership category. What I brought to the *Peer Review of Assessment in Initial Teacher Education* project in my second term as NADLATE Chair was a deeper understanding

Table 6.1 Analysis of academic leadership categories (Juntrasook, 2014) in my lived experience of be(com)ing an academic leader in higher education through NADLATE example

My lived experience of be(com)ing an academic leader in higher education: NADLATE

Leadership as position	Leadership as performance	Leadership as practice	Leadership as professional role model
NADLATE Chair (2017–18) and Associate Dean Teaching and Learning (ADTL)	ensuring the ADTL members are actively engaged in NADLATE	*Peer review of Initial Teacher Education* project	modelling collaborative and dialogic approaches to establish the project
NADLATE Academic Facilitator (2013–14)	transition support to new Steering Group		mentor & support incoming NADLATE Chair and Steering Group
NADLATE (inaugural) Chair (2012) & ADTL	lead the process of establishing NADLATE goals and Terms of Reference	work collaboratively to generate the ways of working & determine project priorities	part of small ADTL group that provided the transition between ACDE's Deans (who gained the grant to establish NADLATE) and the broader ADTL group charged to operationalise the vision into practice
NADLATE member as ADTL (2011–12; 2015–18)		contribute to the NADLATE goals and priority projects	

of what was aspirational yet possible because I had a working knowledge of NADLATE and what we were capable of as a group. Through my deep engagement with the context of Initial Teacher Education and its place within broader emerging accreditation issues, I was able to reflect, inform and transfer vision and strategy to the NADLATE context through the external peer review project. Identifying a meaningful project, I built 'trust credits' (Middlehurst, 2008, p. 336) for when our collaborative project ran into challenges such as the dysfunction of the promised software platform. The project could have been abandoned at that point, but the intensive work to develop common purpose and protocols in the project's Establishing phase had ensured the project team's resilience to keep working, albeit with workaround strategies.

The reflective analysis also affirmed that rather than focus on me being a *leader* (leadership as position), I am more comfortable with exercising *leadership*, which is 'an outcome . . . of practice involving . . . person[s] and non-human artefacts' or leadership as practice (Youngs, 2017, p. 141). However, without being in the leadership as position, that is, an Associate Dean Teaching and Learning, I would not have had the opportunity to undertake the NADLATE Chair role. Therefore, I argue that leadership as position offers greater opportunities to enact other academic leadership categories such as leadership as practice or leadership as professional role model. Yet, if I take a holistic view of my lived experience as leader for teaching and learning, it has been the taking up of distributed leadership opportunities, where I *practised* leadership (i.e. Juntrasook's leadership as practice category) 'safely' because they were bounded in some way (e.g. within a specific time period or context). Such opportunities are akin to the concept of leadership as practice (Raelin, 2016; Youngs, 2017) and allowed me to playfully engage with leadership processes that are relational and respond meaningfully to the dynamism of situational contexts as they arise.

While current thinking about educational leadership in higher education is moving away from a study of personal traits attached to a leader, I want to acknowledge that for me to carry out academic leadership, I do require an ever-changing repertoire of attributes, dispositions, knowledge and skills that I must ascertain to use appropriately for any given situational context. For this reason, I also concur with Raelin (2016) and Middlehurst (2008) that reflection and ongoing formal, non-formal and informal learning is critical to intervene and enhance collaborative leadership through action learning to enable *learning to be* and act purposefully. Be(com)ing an academic leader *for* teaching and learning in higher education is a non-linear trajectory with attention to leadership as practice and collaborative leadership that integrates professional and situated action learning.

Notes

1 www.teqsa.gov.au/
2 For more information on NADLATE's work and governance, visit: www.acde.edu.au/networks-and-partnerships/nadlate/

References

Angelo, T. A. (2000). Transforming departments into productive learning communities. In A. F. Lucas (Ed.), *Leading academic change: Essential roles for department chairs* (pp. 74–89). Jossey-Bass.
Bryman, A. (2007). Effective leadership in higher education: A literature review. *Studies in Higher Education, 32*(6), 693–710.
Clandinin, D. J. (2013). *Engaging in narrative inquiry*. Left Coast Press.

Dickinson, J., Fowler, A., & Griffiths, T.-L. (2020). Pracademics? Exploring transitions and professional identities in higher education. *Studies in Higher Education, 47*(2), 290–304. https://doi.org/10.1080/03075079.2020.1744123

Gallos, J. V., & Bolman, L. G. (2021). *Reframing academic leadership* (2nd ed.). Jossey-Bass.

Juntrasook, A. (2014). 'You do not have to be the boss to be a leader': Contested meanings of leadership in higher education. *Higher Education Research & Development, 33*(1), 19–31.

Korthagen, F. A. J., Kessels, J., Koster, B., Lagerwerf, B., & Wubbels, T. (2001). *Linking practice and theory: The pedagogy of realistic teacher education*. Lawrence Erlbaum Associates.

Legood, A., van der Werff, L., Lee, A., & Den Hartog, D. (2021). A meta-analysis of the role of trust in the leadership-performance relationship. *European Journal of Work and Organisational Psychology, 30*(1), 1–22.

Lucas, A. F. (Ed.). (2000). *Leading academic change: Essential roles for department chairs*. Jossey-Bass.

Marshall, S. J., Orrell, J., Cameron, A., Bosanquet, A., & Thomas, S. (2011). Leading and managing learning and teaching in higher education. *Higher Education Research & Development, 30*(2), 87–103.

Mason, T., & de la Harpe, B. (2020). The state of play of associate deans, learning and teaching, in Australian universities, 30 years on. *Higher Education Research & Development, 39*(3), 532–545.

Middlehurst, R. (2008). Not enough science or not enough learning? Exploring the gaps between leadership theory and practice. *Higher Education Quarterly, 62*(4), 322–339.

Raelin, J. A. (2016). It's not about the leaders: It's about the practice of leadership. *Organizational Dynamics, 45*(2), 124–131.

Youngs, H. (2017). A critical exploration of collaborative and distributed leadership in higher education: Developing an alternative ontology through leadership-as-practice. *Journal of Higher Education Policy and Management, 39*(2), 140–154.

Zeichner, K. (2005). Becoming a teacher educator: A personal perspective. *Teaching and Teacher Education, 21*(2), 117–124.

7 Leading as an international academic
A case study of a casual teaching team

Jasvir Kaur Nachatar Singh

Introduction

In Australia, around 80% of undergraduate teaching is done by casual academic staff (Klopper & Power, 2014). Casual teaching staff are normally on precarious contracts and are there to support the delivery of the teaching that is led by permanent academic staff. I began my university career in Malaysia and experienced being a casual teaching staff in Australia during my PhD studies, where I was employed at various universities in Melbourne, Australia. Upon completion of my PhD, in 2016, I was offered an associate lecturer position (on contract) at the Department of Management and Marketing at La Trobe University. Within two years, I was appointed as a lecturer (on continuing/tenured position) at the Department, and in 2021, I was promoted as a senior lecturer (my journey is further detailed in Singh, 2020).

As a senior lecturer, I led a small teaching team (two to three staff), who were casual staff members in the learning and teaching space. In this case study, I will explore the issues I have had in leading this team based on my leadership approach, particularly as an international academic. International academics are individuals born overseas, 'educated and enculturated in one system of education and currently teaching and researching in another' (Walker, 2015, p. 61).

My experiences comprise leading teaching teams for subject redevelopment to improve learning and teaching in higher education. The chapter is organised in five key sections. Section 1 explores the learning and teaching leadership in higher education underpinned by informal leadership roles, followed by a section unpacking the challenges that I faced as a leader in the learning and teaching process. Section 3 presents strategies I personally adopted that were successful in my learning and teaching leadership. Section 4 offers recommendations and lessons learned based on my informal leadership role as a subject coordinator. The final section provides a conclusion.

Background to the casual teaching team case

In recognition of my extensive teaching experience, I was provided with the opportunity early on at La Trobe University to be a subject coordinator, a non-formal leadership role relating to learning and teaching as well as administrative. This is an informal leadership position as every teaching staff member at La Trobe University is expected to take on this role, without assigned formalised power. It involves working directly with students to inspire and motivate them, supporting and encouraging tutors, students and colleagues associated with the subject, curriculum design and delivery (Debowski & Blake, 2004; Roberts et al., 2012) to promote the student learning experience and satisfaction. This is part of our workload as teaching staff members. According to Roberts et al. (2012), we are regarded as leaders of learning in proactively and professionally delivering and modelling 'scholarly teaching approaches to students and staff that reflect contemporary disciplinary content and practice' (p. 5). Largely this role is not considered as a leadership position in the formal and traditional sense, where it influences the culture and learning and teaching in strategic ways (Marshall et al., 2011) at a broader management level.

Although I was in a junior position as an associate lecturer, in 2016 the opportunity to lead subjects and a teaching team as a subject coordinator was provided to me by my head of department. I was given the task to co-lead in re-designing my first subject called 'Leadership: What Matters' and then was offered to be in charge of the subject and lead several other human resource-related subjects for several years. As the subject coordinator, I had to mentor and coordinate casual teaching staff members alongside designing and re-designing curriculum, developing teaching materials, addressing all student queries, moderating marking and presenting overall student results.

I align myself with the overarching definition of leadership as the ability to influence followers to achieve a common goal (Kouzes & Posner, 2002). Smith and Hughey (2006) write that 'leadership has always been a somewhat ambiguous concept: there appears to be no single, concise definition of it that encompasses all of its various manifestations' (p. 157). For me, I took my leadership of the casual teaching staff to be based on Debowski and Blake (2004), who define learning and teaching leadership as 'where an individual seeks to influence the teaching practice of others' (p. 2) and highlight that this kind of leadership occurs at all levels of the university, from the Pro-Vice-Chancellor (Academic) through to the Subject Coordinator (Roberts et al., 2012).

Challenges of leading a teaching team as an international academic

In this section, I am focusing on the challenges that I faced in leading a teaching team under my supervision in 2016. As an international academic, I faced significant challenges in understanding the complexity of Australian learning and leading cultures as I had no experience in leading teaching staff in the Australian context prior to 2016. Since I was educated in Malaysia and worked in a Malaysian university as a professional staff member, I had a hierarchical mindset. According to Hofstede (1980), hierarchical power difference in Malaysia is high and in Australia very low. From my Malaysian university cultural context, this meant there should be a power distance between me (the subject coordinator) and my casual teaching staff members. I had the hierarchical mindset that my casual teaching staff members needed to follow and respect what I said and deliver the subject materials and content according to my preparation. I demonstrated task-oriented leader behaviours where I was concerned to get the job done, instead of establishing relationships or people-oriented behaviours (Kahn & Katz, 1960). Consequently, in the Australian university context, this behaviour of mine did not foster high group productivity among my teaching staff members (Kahn & Katz, 1960). In employing the task-oriented leadership approach, I adopted an authoritarian attitude: I took control of all decisions, made choices based on my own ideas and judgements and hardly involved my teaching staff members in the learning and teaching process (Chukwusa, 2018). Specifically, there was a lack of discussion with my teaching staff members to improve the teaching delivery and meet the learning expectations of students. I used to have meetings prior to the start and during a semester to guide or explain to my teaching team on teaching-related matters. I assumed that they were able to grasp all the instructions provided to them in these meetings.

Early in my teaching career, I observed that my casual teaching staff members had the mindset of questioning and being upfront with the subject coordinator. I found this personally confrontational and disrespectful, as in the Malaysian culture we just follow the manager at our workplaces. I am from a collectivist culture, which, for me, means I value interconnectedness and group membership over individual pursuit. Thus, being a Malaysian, I viewed leadership effectiveness as a long-term goal resulting from my loyalty and commitment and not questioning the leader's authority – this is in contrast to Australia's individualistic culture (Hofstede, 1980). Jogulu (2010) further argued that Malaysians 'tend to avoid direct debate and get through tasks quietly because leaders set clear expectations of how roles should be enacted' (p. 713). Malaysian leaders are 'viewed as authority figures in organisations and open discussions on conflicts are not encouraged' (Jogulu, 2010, p. 713). Hence, I was taken aback with all the questions I received, although the questions were valid, and staff just wanted to improvise the subject material and delivery accordingly. Frankly, I was unhappy with this situation as I struggled to understand – 'Why can't they just follow what I say and do it without discussion?' I could not relate to Jogulu's (2010) explanation that Australian culture promotes behaviours such as participative, consultative and co-cooperativeness in making decisions with the leader(s).

New directions for leadership of a teaching team as an international academic

Once I sensed low teaching morale among my teaching staff, it took me over a year to reorient my hierarchical mindset to suit the Australian teaching environment. I sought assistance from my teaching mentors who I worked with when I was a casual staff member while pursuing my PhD studies. They are Australian-born, and they were ready to help me transform my leadership approach and mindset in leading my team, in accordance with the Australian context. I usually met them over coffee sessions which were before, during and after a semester ended to seek their suggestions and guidance based on issues that I faced. They would always remind me to reflect on their actions when I was their casual teaching staff member. I learned to adopt and adapt, learn, relearn and unlearn my leadership approaches accordingly. Most importantly, I did not feel intimidated or shy in the face of their honest feedback because they did not judge me. They knew that my actions and behaviours were underpinned by my Malaysian culture, values and ways of doing things differently, which had proven less effective in Australian academia.

As an international academic, I have to first acknowledge that there appears to be a more 'flat' system in Australia in which subject coordinators and casual teaching staff members are on a similar level playing field for teaching, which provides more autonomy for casual teaching staff. In order to overcome this barrier, I learned to be open to constructive feedback provided by my casual teaching staff members. At first, it was difficult for me to grasp the 'flat' hierarchical system in Australia, but in order to manage my relationship with my casual teaching staff members, I started using their feedback for the purpose of providing excellent learning experiences to students. Over time, I can say that I have fostered good relationships with my casual teaching staff members and we work together in designing subject delivery.

My change in leadership approach is reflected in my strategies when I meet with the teaching team (at least five times in a semester). The first meeting would be before the start of the semester; we discuss the content, delivery method, materials, assessments, just so that all views are incorporated into our teaching and delivery. The second meeting is usually after the submission of the first assessment. In this meeting, we moderate our marking and deliberate on the assessment – what needs to change in the future and what worked. During the semester, the casual teaching staff members and I meet up after the submissions of the second and third assignments, again to moderate our marking. The final meeting is where we get together and reflect on the subject content, delivery, assessment and student expectations so that we are able to either change or keep the current teaching-related practices for the next delivery. This meeting is an important one for me as the leader of the subject (i.e. subject coordinator) as I actively listen to my casual staff members' barriers in teaching, teaching strategies employed by them which are sustainable and can be adopted and adapted by all of us, as well as successes that came their way which we all can celebrate together. This reflective exercise is a very important and integral part where we all then revise accordingly the subject delivery for the next semester. Underpinning these actions, I have demonstrated leadership qualities where I have been an inclusive, adaptative, consultative and respectful leader.

As a testament to these leadership qualities and relationship-oriented behaviour style, most of the subjects have improved in their Student Feedback on Subject (SFS) evaluation each year under my leadership. For instance, students have rated the *Human Resource Development* subject's overall teaching evaluation improved from 3.92/5.00 in 2019 to 4.30/5.00 in 2020; similarly, *Evaluate and Negotiate* subject has improved from 3.57/5.00 in 2019 to 3.76 in 2020 and 3.79/5.00 in 2021, despite COVID-19. Some of the qualitative comments provided by students on teaching staff members include:

> *[Casual staff member 1] was the best teacher I have ever had, so helpful and engaging and made the subject so enjoyable.*
>
> (Student Feedback Survey, 2020)

> *The subject coordinator and my teacher for the subject, was absolutely wonderful! She was both positive and patient! A great teacher whom I hope to have again sometime in the future! The subject is engaging and interesting*!
>
> (Student Feedback Survey, 2020)

Reflection on my evolving leadership approach

Just when I thought that I had successfully built an excellent teaching team, the COVID-19 pandemic hit Australia in early 2020. My learning and teaching leadership was much more evident during COVID-19, where we had to pivot our face-to-face teaching to online within a week. My experiences of pivoting to online learning and teaching are captured in my recent journal publications (Singh, 2021; Singh & Chowdhury, 2021).

As a learning and teaching leader in a pandemic with no positional authority per se, I have adopted a less hierarchical higher education leadership approach, with elements of a distributed, collaborative approach to leadership (Jones et al., 2012). According to Parker (2008), non-positional leaders described 'leadership as distributed, networked, inclusive and action-oriented' (pp. 21–22). The focus of distributive leadership is on 'collective collaboration rather than individual power and control' to build leadership capacity in the learning and teaching space (Jones et al., 2012, p. 67). For me, collegiality and inclusiveness matter, as I am a firm believer in learning from my casual teaching staff, who have a wealth of teaching skills and knowledge. As stated previously, we used to have at least five meetings throughout the semester, but during COVID-19, I lost count of the constant meetings that I had with my casual teaching staff. These additional meetings were held to inform them about the new delivery mode (online teaching), curriculum re-design reflecting online mode, seeking ways to promote students' engagement in the online learning, and facilitating online assessment. Therefore, in the subject meetings, we deliberated and developed together online learning and teaching strategies such as utilising innovative online teaching tools and sharing of online teaching knowledge and experiences to address the challenges that we faced as a teaching team which included international academics (Singh & Chowdhury, 2021).

Recommendations and lessons learned

As an international academic leading casual teaching staff, I acknowledge that my actions were underpinned by my home-country culture and values. Therefore, the most important thing to learn here is to adapt and adopt the host-country culture and recognise the culture or systems that other teaching staff are working within. This is not to necessarily assimilate but, rather, to overcome barriers and achieve goals. Some of the recommendations and lessons learned about teaching and learning leadership from my case study presented in the chapter are listed in the following paragraphs.

1) Mentor

I would strongly suggest to academics, especially international academics who are new to the teaching system in a university, to locate teaching mentor(s). I was blessed to have two teaching mentors who were Australian-born. I learned from them the Australian way of doing things, which helped me to understand Australian workplace culture as well as leadership approaches and to recognise the issues that casual staff may have. Thomas and Malau-Aduli (2013) further explain that Australian-born mentors provide international academics with vital local professional support, such as directing them towards gaining relevant resources and knowledge, as well as offering guidance in navigating their career path in academia.

2) Teaching-related leadership professional development

When I joined La Trobe University in 2016, there was limited professional development, especially in developing learning and teaching leadership. Therefore, I did not attend any teaching-related leadership training, and I struggled with the challenges mentioned earlier in this chapter. Moving forward several years, La Trobe University currently offers numerous learning and teaching leadership workshops to all staff members. I would strongly suggest that (international) academics participate if this professional development is offered at your university. Professional development courses will enable international academics to further understand the host university's leadership values, beliefs and preferences, such as specific types of leadership behaviour applicable to the work environment. Participation in such training courses will also develop (international) academics' leadership effectiveness; by 'comparing and contrasting the number of cultural frameworks of leadership styles, more holistic understanding can be attained' (Paulienė, 2012, p. 95).

3) Acknowledging differing leadership approaches

As (international) academics, we need to increase our awareness that culture does play an underpinning role in influencing our leadership behaviours (Jogulu, 2010). Without this awareness, we will face significant difficulties in our leadership journey in the host country. Jogulu (2010) proposed that it is vital 'to recognise that different cultures maintain different sets of norms and beliefs towards leadership styles because they reflect different concepts of how reality should be viewed and practised' (p. 716).

Conclusion

As an international academic, it is harder to showcase your leadership abilities due to cultural complexities. Specifically, I had the mindset of a task-oriented leader where I was directive. It is a one-way street leadership approach where the leader will lay down the rules, and the team members will just have to follow them. It took me over a year to understand this leadership approach was destructive to my team members' motivation levels, particularly those who were casual staff. Therefore, with the help of my teaching mentors, I was able to change my leadership approach to be more inclusive, open to constructive feedback and action-oriented. As I am genuinely passionate about the learning and teaching scholarship space, I constantly think about and find ways to innovate in my subjects and lead my casual team members to achieve teaching excellence, whilst also seeking to motivate as well as inspire students to achieve high engagement and satisfaction levels.

References

Chukwusa, J. (2018). Autocratic leadership style: Obstacle to success in academic libraries. *Library Philosophy and Practice* (pp. 1–11). https://digitalcommons.unl.edu/libphilprac/2019/

Debowski, S., & Blake, V. (2004). *The developmental needs of higher education academic leaders in encouraging effective teaching and learning.* Paper presented at the 13th Annual Teaching Learning Forum, Murdoch University, Perth.

Hofstede, G. (1980). *Culture's consequences: International differences in work-related values* (1st ed.). SAGE.

Jogulu, U. D. (2010). Culturally-linked leadership styles. *Leadership & Organization Development Journal, 31*(8), 705–719. https://doi.org/10.1108/01437731011094766

Jones, S., Lefoe, G., Harvey, M., & Ryland, K. (2012). Distributed leadership: A collaborative framework for academics, executives and professionals in higher education. *Journal of Higher Education Policy and Management, 34*(1), 67–78. https://doi.org/10.1080/1360080X.2012.642334

Kahn, R., & Katz, D. (1960). Leadership practices in relation to productivity and morale. In D. Cartwright & A. Zander (Eds.), *Group dynamics: Research and theory* (2nd ed.). Row Paterson.

Klopper, C. J., & Power, B. M. (2014). The casual approach to teacher education: What effect does casualisation have for Australian university teaching? *Australian Journal of Teacher Education* (Online), *39*(4), 101–114. http://dx.doi.org/10.14221/ajte.2014v39n4.1

Kouzes, J., & Posner, B. (2002). *The leadership challenge* (3rd ed.). Jossey-Bass.

Marshall, S., Orrell, J., Cameron, A., Bosanquet, A., & Thomas, S. (2011). Leading and managing learning and teaching in higher education. *Higher Education Research & Development, 30*(2), 87–103. https://doi.org/10.1080/07294360.2010.512631

Parker, L. (2008). *Leadership for excellence in learning and teaching in Australian higher education: Review of the Australian learning and teaching council (ALTC) programme 2006–2008*. www.altc.edu.au/carrick/webdav/site/carricksite/users/siteadmin/publi c/review_leadershipprogramme_parker_2008.pdf

Paulienė, R. (2012). Transforming leadership styles and knowledge sharing in a multicultural context. *Business, Management and Economics Engineering, 10*(1), 91–109. https://doi.org/10.3846/bme.2012.08

Roberts, S. A., Butcher, L., Brooker, M. R., Cummings, R., Schibeci, R., Jones, S., & Phillips, R. (2012). *Clarifying, developing and valuing the role of unit coordinators as informal leaders of learning in higher education*. Australian Learning and Teaching Council.

Singh, J. K. N. (2020). Why should I walk the same career development pathways as everyone else? In T. L. H. Nghia, T. Pham, M. Tomlinson, K. Medica, & C. Thompson (Eds.), *Developing and utilizing employability capitals: Graduates' strategies across labour markets* (pp. 211–225). Taylor & Francis.

Singh, J. K. N. (2021). Online learning and best teaching practices in COVID-19 environment: A case study in Australia. *SEAMEO Journal 2020 Special Issue, 2*, 47–53. www.seameo.org/img/Publications/SEAMES/SEAMEO%20Journal%202020%20%20V2%20Special%20Issue.pdf

Singh, J. K. N., & Chowdhury, H. (2021). Early-career international academics' learning and teaching experiences during COVID-19 in Australia: A collaborative autoethnography. *Journal of University Teaching and Learning Practice, 18*(5), 1–17. https://doi.org/10.53761/1.18.5.12

Smith, B. L., & Hughey, A. W. (2006). Leadership in higher education – its evolution and potential: A unique role facing critical challenges. *Industry and Higher Education, 20*(3), 157–163. https://doi.org/10.5367/000000006777690972

Thomas, S. L., & Malau-Aduli, B. S. (2013). New international academics' narratives of cross-cultural transition. *International Journal of Higher Education, 2*(2), 35–52. https://doi.org/10.5430/ijhe.v2n2p35

Walker, P. (2015). The globalisation of higher education and the sojourner academic: Insights into challenges experienced by newly appointed international academic staff in a UK university. *Journal of Research in International Education, 14*(1), 61–74. https://doi.org/10.1177/1475240915571032

8 A leadership quest in teaching and learning
A case study of building capability and competency

Barbara C. Panther

I see my professional trajectory in leadership as a quest. Everyone loves a quest – where a hero and their entourage go out into the world to complete a task. Along the way, their view of the world changes as they are exposed to new experiences and challenges. Their interactions with those they meet cause them to rethink what they know about the world they are in and how they should respond. Critical moments occur which cause the hero to pause and reflect on the context in which they find themselves, the needs of the situation and what they need to learn to successfully complete the task at hand. This is a tale that does not occur on a lonely road; it is populated with people, institutions and circumstances that shape the travellers just as they must shape themselves to traverse it. Such questing calls for curiosity, humility, creativity and a great deal of reflection.

I see my adventures in teaching and learning in higher education as such a quest – this chapter considers my personal trajectory towards better learning and teaching, which began long before I held a formal leadership role. The path I have travelled, across 30 years, was from a small faculty in a regional campus to a central leadership role in one of the largest universities in Australia. Along the way – my quest for excellence in learning and teaching crossed borders, moved from small to ever larger communities, interacting with people with diverse needs and problems, with ever-expanding goals.

As I travelled, my companions on the quest changed, the community I was championing differed, and my sphere of influence grew ever larger. Each challenge brought critical moments which required me to reflect on my role, on my core competencies and capabilities, and to find ways to build new skills. This chapter is a case study about building capacity and competence at a personal and institutional level. I will reflect on key lessons from that quest – lessons that have developed from those critical incidents that caused me to pause and reflect on how I would act, on who I needed with me, on how I would influence those around me, and on how I would build my own capabilities to accomplish the task at hand.

A leadership quest in teaching and learning 67

The academic leadership capability framework

Such a leadership quest requires more than the knowledge and skills (competencies) required for the completion of tasks. Leaders also need intellectual, personal and interpersonal skills (capabilities) to respond in effective ways to situations as they arise. These capabilities are often not made explicit in the process of gaining a leadership role but are critically important for successful leadership.

Scott et al.'s (2008) academic leadership capability model provides a useful guide for such a leadership quest because it brings together both the competencies and the capabilities needed by leaders of teaching and learning (shown in Figure 8.1). Scott et al. (2008) emphasise that while competencies such as knowledge of how higher education operates or what makes good teaching and learning are necessary, they are not sufficient for leaders to be effective, they also need particular emotional intelligence capabilities (see Figure 8.1) such as: personal capabilities include the ability for self-regulation, decisiveness and commitment; interpersonal capabilities encompass influence and empathy for others and the cognitive capabilities recognise the need for diagnosis, strategic thinking, flexibility and responsiveness. These are underpinned by two core competencies (generic and role-specific) which are the skills and knowledge required to undertake a role.

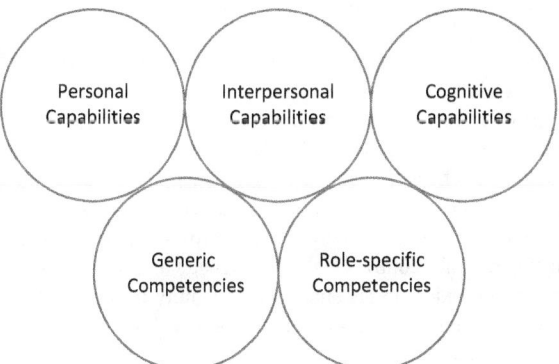

Figure 8.1 The Academic Leadership model (adapted from Scott et al., 2008, p. 18)

I will attempt to share critical moments in my professional trajectory through the lens of Scott et al.'s (2008) capabilities and competencies in hopes of shining a light on the unseen moments of contemporary leadership in higher education. Hopefully, this will provide others with some tools for their own quest to build personal, interpersonal and intellectual capacity.

Quest challenge 1: knowing teaching and learning as a discipline

This quest began at a regional university campus where I worked as a sessional lecturer in chemistry – teaching both on campus and online. The students were the focus of my activities. My credibility as a leader came from my competencies in chemistry and online pedagogies, and my willingness to share my ideas with my colleagues (Fields et al., 2019). Like many on such a journey, as my skills increased, I became recognised as an expert in online learning, first in my faculty and then across my campus. My sphere of influence was my team and my faculty, and my focus was on sharing my knowledge of online learning with my peers with a goal of impacting directly on the experience of their students.

As I shared my practice and experiences more widely, I quickly identified gaps in my understanding of teaching and learning and in my lack of credibility as I moved to influence those outside of my discipline. Although I was very competent in the use of technology in teaching science and had good links with the chemistry education community within Australia, I had little understanding of pedagogy and learning theory. I did not know the discourse of this broader community. I found myself at a loss to understand the methodologies and language used by my education-based colleagues – I had never heard of 'pedagogy' and did not understand their qualitative research methods. I did not have the language to articulate or evaluate my practice in this new world. Therefore, I enrolled in postgraduate education courses, first a Graduate Certificate in Higher Education, followed by a Master's degree in Educational Technology. This enabled me to explore how to evidence and evaluate my practice and built a strong core knowledge of how to effectively use technology in teaching and learning.

The impact of these two learning experiences was profound – I was able to communicate in the language of higher education pedagogy, had a deeper understanding of scholarship, and evidence which informed teaching; I began to think deeply about my own discipline understandings and biases related to how to teach effectively. These were the role-specific competencies that I needed (Scott et al., 2008). This new language and understanding allowed me to engage in wider circles and build capability in others, and to bring a multidisciplinary lens to my informal leadership roles.

Quest challenge 2: Knowing teaching and learning in other disciplines

My first formal leadership role was as the Associate Dean, Teaching and Learning (ADTL) in a faculty. The ADTL role is, in many ways, an ambiguous one, and often the priorities and activities are very different across different contexts. This was my first experience of setting my own agenda as to how we would build teaching capability and quality within the faculty, a task that was initially daunting. I did not have a map to show where I was headed, just a vague destination. While my sphere of influence was now at the university level, my focus was firmly on championing the needs of my colleagues within the faculty – a new community, who I did not yet know and understand. My task was to find ways to convince these diverse academics to embrace faculty-level initiatives such as curriculum redevelopment, teaching practice improvements and the introduction of online learning for some who had always taught face-to-face. I also had the weighty responsibility and privilege of representing their needs and challenges in faculty and university decision-making.

Early in my new role, I ran a workshop for the faculty about writing effective exams – a topic that I thought I knew well. In this critical moment, I saw the vast differences in the way each of the disciplines in the faculty had approached the development of assessment – I realised that what I saw as good practice from my experience, or from my engagement with literature, was not necessarily what these teachers knew from the cultural norms of their discipline. Each discipline had its own 'folk pedagogies' (Olson & Bruner, 1996) – implicit and tacit knowledge about teaching and learning which is gained through personal experience within a discipline. Once again, I found myself without the language or the understanding of the culture of the world I had entered. My first challenge to build this understanding was to get to know this pedagogy. I decided to explore my new community – visiting every academic individually to find out about their challenges and successes, and to build personal relationships which enabled me to see synergies across their activities and to understand the broad range of individual teaching contexts and approaches. I made myself available to them: 'Being accessible is critical to identifying small problems before they become big ones' (Scott et al., 2008, p. 107). This also allowed them to get to know me and understand my motivations and experience in teaching and learning.

The social and interpersonal capabilities from Scott et al.'s (2008) framework were critical to being effective in building the required competencies. Being empathetic and responsive enabled me to understand their practice and find ways to lead and motivate them effectively. Ramsden (1998) highlighted the importance of emotional intelligence for leaders when influencing the practice of others – in particular being able to listen, encouraging initiative and helping staff to reflect on, and grow their practice.

But I did not just need to get to know those I was championing – I also needed to understand the motivation of those I was trying to influence. I met with colleagues in other faculties, in governance and in central units, to understand how their work would impact on the faculty and what they were trying to achieve in their own roles.

This relationship building took time and effort but was highly rewarding in allowing me to develop my understanding of the larger environment in which

I was now travelling and allowing my community to understand me and how I could help them. Ramsden (1998) refers to this capability of being *plugged in* as 'being a person who knows what is going on' (p. 87). These relationships have also helped me in future quests – building relationships may not pay dividends immediately, but when you get stuck, these are people you can call on for assistance. This leadership as relationship approach (Popper, 2004) is critical for effective leadership – to respond to challenges, a leader must first fully understand the needs and motivations of the circles in which they work. Building trust among my community and ensuring I was accessible were critical in giving them the confidence to come to me with their problems, knowing that I would represent their needs in decision-making.

Quest challenge 3: Knowing when I needed companions for the quest

Often quests are not solo endeavours. Along the journey we collect fellow seekers – those who can adventure with us, with skills we have not yet developed, like-minded souls to encourage us when the way is not clear, and critical friends who help us to make balanced decisions.

Being tasked with the development of the University's strategic learning and teaching plan for the next five years was one such moment when I needed to build a team to reach a goal. I understood that the plan needed to reflect a range of points of view to be successful and I had no experience in the process of developing strategy. So, I asked an expert in strategic planning to quest with me. Together, we identified and worked with all of those who were important to, and invested in, the implementation of the plan. We then brought this community together to develop an owned, consolidated plan of action for the next five years.

He helped me to understand the need to focus on the larger picture and not get lost in the alleyways of school and faculty-specific needs – to listen carefully to the stories of the resistors and the over-enthusiastic. A key learning for me from this was the value of really listening to what others had to say – particularly the resistors. After I had completed what I thought was an inclusive, collaborative planning process, one of the stakeholders told me that he did not feel like he had been listened to. This moment gave me pause to think about my own role in bringing the resistors along for the journey. Fullan (2001) sees appreciating resistance as a 'remarkable discovery' (p. 65). Dissenters are often a source of new ideas and can identify the barriers that must be overcome in any project. Scott et al. (2008) encourage us to ensure the resistors are part of the shaping and implementation of any change project in teaching and learning (p. 106).

Formal professional learning opportunities had always served me well in the early part of my career, but informal opportunities to learn from others have been critical in the later parts of my travels. 'Just as higher education student learning is a profoundly social experience, with informal peer support being a key factor in retention and productive learning, so it is for academic leaders' (Scott et al., 2008, p. 107). I looked to networks within the university and beyond. I engaged with learning leaders from other faculties in a regular learning community. We used this informal network of fellow travellers to share and learn from each other's experiences within the role. We shared our knowledge of our disciplines to help each other establish a broader base of understanding. I spent time really listening to those with other views. I joined several national networks for leaders in teaching and learning, and met and learned from learning leaders from across the sector, building my understanding of the diversity of the role and approaches that were being taken by others.

Quest challenge 4: Knowing and influencing the culture of an organisation

When my journey took me to a role in a central teaching and learning unit in a large university, my quest became more difficult – to influence the culture of an organisation. My mission was to build a culture in which teaching and learning are demonstrably valued in the institution and to recognise and build the capability of teaching teams. One critical moment early in this role was recognising the challenge in leaving an old culture behind. The history of the team and the university, and the way things had always been done, pervaded my colleagues' approach to their work. I came into the role with a range of ideas about how to make this change, but first I had to step back and understand the culture that existed. Scott et al. (2008) encourage us to remember that 'culture counts: that change, like learning, is a profoundly social experience, and that one's peer group is an important source of motivation (or demotivation) and support' (p. 85).

This organisation was large, and I could no longer develop personal relationships as deeply as I once did. But I now had a team around me to help me on this quest – and a team that I was responsible for. My responsibility for my new companions was different – it was my job to give control and agency to those around me, to share responsibility and authority with them and create opportunities for them to develop and shine. But first, I needed to spend time painting a picture of where we were headed, to help them to question their 'sacred cows' in teaching and learning (Ramsden, 1998, p. 87), and to convince them of the value of the programmes I wanted to create. Like many embarking on a quest, my companions came from diverse backgrounds with a range of strengths and perspectives to be negotiated. My role was to bring those perspectives and strengths together in our work. Our quest required both a map – a shared vision of where we were heading – and a clear picture of what success looked like (Scott et al., 2008, p. 107).

My circle had expanded even further to include not just academics, but professional staff in a range of roles that deliver, enable and lead teaching and learning within the organisation. I now had to represent, advocate for and influence a very diverse teaching and learning staff. Motivators for staff engagement differ greatly for those in different roles. 'Effective leaders read what mix of intrinsic and extrinsic motivators are likely to work with particular people and match an appropriate strategy' (Scott et al., 2008, p. 108). Together with my team, I identified and made relationships with key people across the university to understand what those motivations might be and how I could engage these staff in our quest. I worked with my team to model the culture we wanted to see. We celebrated achievements that may have seemed small but signified a positive change in 'the way things are done around here' to keep our eye on what was important. Culture change is a long game and I have grown comfortable with this.

Epilogue

So, what advice would I give to others embarking on their leadership quest? My engagement with reflective practice through the Advance HE Fellowship programme was a turning point in the way that I made sense of my experiences as a leader. This process of applying a very specific reflective lens to my practice allowed me to think deeply on each of my experiences in leadership – what my role was, what my motivations were, the impact of my actions and what led me to these actions in the first place. Scott et al. (2008) identify that understanding our personal strengths and limitations is one of the important personal capabilities in leadership. I was challenged to think about my leadership failures: the project that failed because I did not clearly articulate a purpose; the resources created that were never used because I did not take the time to understand the needs of my community; the programmes that my colleagues did not engage with. Failures, like resistors, are a tool for refining and relearning how to lead. On every quest, we need to make time to think and reflect on our progress, on our successes as well as our failures, celebrate each small victory, and continually check that we are still on the path to our destination.

I would also draw from, and add to, the practical actions recommended by Scott et al. (2008) for how to put the personal, interpersonal, and cognitive capabilities into practice as a leader of learning and teaching.

Firstly, arm yourself with the knowledge and skills you need to undertake your quest. These will be ever-evolving, and continuous professional learning is vital in the leadership journey. Read widely, find ways to build your capabilities in the personal, interpersonal and cognitive skills you will need on each stage of your adventure. Learn the language you need to build your credibility in each new place.

Secondly, get to know the community you are working with and for – spend time listening to their stories, put yourself in their shoes and find ways to bring them together with shared goals. Try to understand their motivations and their pedagogies.

Thirdly, build a reciprocal network of companions who can travel with you. Some of these folk will come and go as the nature of your adventures change, but some will stay with you for the whole journey. Use them to make sense of your challenges, identify the stumbling blocks on your path and test your ideas. Learn from their experience and share yours with them.

Fourthly, make time to understand the culture in which you are working. Recognise how important it is. Set clear expectations for your projects and be explicit about what success looks like. Share this information with your companions and your community. This becomes even more important when you are sending out others to tackle tasks on your behalf.

Finally, know yourself and where you are headed. Make time to reflect on who you are as a leader and how you want to lead. Recognise your role in setting the culture of your organisation – demonstrate, through your actions, the culture you would like to see.

As I continue this journey of leadership, I know there will be further quests to conquer and other critical moments that will cause me to reflect on my capabilities and capacity. My journey now leads me to help others in their quests – to find their road to learning and teaching leadership. 'Leadership is not a destination . . . rather it is an ongoing journey that requires adaptation, transformation and change' (Bolden et al., 2008, p. 4).

I would like to acknowledge all of those who have travelled with me on my quest, particularly Adam Baker, Danni McCarthy and Lauren Hansen, who helped me to shape this story.

References

Bolden, R., Petrov, G., & Gosling, J. (2008). *Developing collective leadership in higher education. Final Report.* Leadership Foundation for Higher Education. www.advance-he.ac.uk/knowledge-hub/developing-collective-leadership-higher-education

Fields, J., Kenny, N. A., & Mueller, R. A. (2019). Conceptualizing educational leadership in an academic development program. *International Journal for Academic Development, 24*(3), 218–231. http://doi.org/10.1080/1360144X.2019.1570211

Fullan, M. (2001). *Leading in a culture of change.* Jossey-Bass.

Olson, D. R., & Bruner, J. S. (1996). Folk psychology and folk pedagogy. In D. R. Olson & N. Torrance (Eds.), *The handbook of education and human development: New models of learning, teaching and schooling* (pp. 9–27). Blackwell Publishing.

Popper, M. (2004). Leadership as Relationship. *Journal for the Theory of Social Behaviour, 34*, 107–125. https://doi.org/10.1111/j.0021-8308.2004.00238.x

Ramsden, P. (1998). *Learning to lead in higher education*. Routledge.
Scott, G., Coates, H., & Anderson, M. (2008). *Learning leaders in times of change: Academic leadership capabilities for Australian higher education*. University of Western Sydney and Australian Council for Educational Research. https://research.acer.edu.au/cgi/viewcontent.cgi?article=1001&context=higher_education

Part III
Implications for practice

9 Conclusion

Perspectives on teaching and learning leadership in higher education: implications for practice

Josephine Lang and Namrata Rao

> *Walker, your footsteps*
>
> Walker, your footsteps
> Are the road, and nothing more.
> Walker, there is no road,
> the road is made by walking.
> Walking you make the road,
> and turning to look behind
> you see the path you never
> again will step upon.
> Walker, there is no road,
> only foam trails on the sea.

Antonio Machado, Proverbs and Songs #29: ["Walker, your footsteps"] from *Border of a Dream: Selected Poems*, translated by Willis Barnstone. Copyright © 2004 by the Heirs of Antonio Machado. English translation copyright © 2004 by Willis Barnstone. Reprinted with the permission of The Permission Company, LLC on behalf of Copper Canyon Press, coppercanyonpress.org.

Introduction

The case studies of teaching and learning leadership shared in Part II of the book present the multiplicity of voices cast in the higher education landscape. The narratives provide insights gained from the lived experiences of leadership and, through the act of sharing, they reveal the diverse opportunities for leading quality teaching and learning in higher education. The stories told add colour, light and shade to such leadership. You will have likely noticed that the chapter authors made meaning of their leadership case studies through the lenses of a variety of theoretical framings, which unveils the complexity of teaching and learning leadership in higher education. This is not an unusual phenomenon in the discipline of leadership theory due to its increasing complexity that 'defies reductive definition, offering a plurality of often contradictory models and theories' (Smith, 2022, p. 102). The analyses of the various case studies included in this book highlighted commonalities between the various narratives; these key themes have been indicated in the next section of this chapter.

Commonality of themes across the case studies

Leadership as change

A dominant theme for each case study author is **leadership as change**. In the shared narratives of their case studies, chapter authors spoke of the changes attributed to their own personal professional learning and practice during their leadership to create change to improve learning and teaching within the organisation. Learning is an expression of change, transitioning from one state to another. It is perhaps, then, not surprising that **leadership as change for personal professional learning** is seen by chapter authors as critical to developing leadership capabilities and their leadership. Frequently, their professional growth and development was deliberate and intentional, and involved intrapersonal reflection on their professional identity and beliefs through the act of 'noticing', which is learning from experience (Smith, 2022). Hence, the chapter authors make meaning of their lived experience through their reflective practices, becoming 'a researcher in the practice context . . . [to] construct a new theory of the unique case' (Schön, 1983, p. 68). Regularly, the chapter authors discussed the need to question their assumptions and change their practice as they spoke of their learning, *un*learning and *re*learning. While sometimes these un/re/learnings were solitary, there were frequent practices of learning from the rich diversity of peers and mentors, as well as the scholarship of teaching and learning. The significance of *leadership as change for personal professional learning* is to create spaces for self-awareness and deep reflection in leadership contexts. The consequential understanding from such introspective work is a critical understanding and dimension of teaching and learning leadership to appreciate the personal values that drive their passion and authenticity for improving teaching and learning within their organisation (Quinlan, 2020). Thus, the *learning leader* is critical to teaching and learning leadership; as also discussed by Wendy Patton,

> leadership knowledge is developmental and evolutionary, requiring continual refinement, with experience acting as a scaffold and even perhaps an incubator as leaders develop their own nuanced skills and perspectives, and make sense of the ongoing interpersonal and social interactions to form them.
>
> (Patton, 2021, pp. 123–124)

As each of the book's case studies has demonstrated in Part II, teaching and learning leadership is intricately interwoven with change of practice in or across multiple higher education institutions. This highlights *leadership as change from an organisational perspective*. To improve the quality of teaching and learning within higher education, Michael Harris and Roxanne Cullen (2010) argue that teaching and learning leadership is about changing the paradigm that governs leadership actions from the old instructional paradigm to the new learner-centred paradigm. They assert that leadership within higher education must be disrupted and shift towards a learning organisation and take on the principles of a learner-centred paradigm, which means leaders 'will adopt practices that are similar to those of the learner-centred teacher' (Harris & Cullen, 2010,

Table 9.1 Competing paradigms informing teaching and learning leadership (adapted from Harris & Cullen, 2010, Chapters 2 and 3)

Instructional Paradigm (old) principles	Learner-Centred Paradigm (new) principles
Fosters divisiveness among all constituents but most negatively between administration and faculty	Balance of power – creating community through sharing power and control
Functions under the assumption that control is necessary; power is with the authoritative figure (e.g. teacher or leader)	Function of content – creating relevance by focusing on what the learner (or staff) learns as opposed to what the knowledge is to be disseminated; prior knowledge and learning are important to understand (from teacher or leader perspective)
Knowledge is a quantifiable commodity & is owned by the discipline (or the gatekeeper of the discipline, that is, teacher or leader)	Role of the teacher (leader): Leaders assuming roles akin to the learner-centred teacher who is described as a facilitator, designer or guide
Devalues individuality and creativity	Responsibility for learning: Fostering a climate for learning by creating community
Operates on a factory model of learning	Assessment and evaluation: Using assessment (or evaluation) to monitor ongoing learning (or work) and gauge effectiveness; uses an adaptive approach to assessment and evaluation where problem-solving requires leaders to take a broader view of the issues and study the organisational or individual values within the situated context of the workplace
Prefers competition to collaboration and fosters isolation	Requires collaboration – and co-design of the learning or work
Results in organisational fragmentation	Result in organisational integration
Fosters dualistic thinking and technical problem solving	Fosters more integrated thinking and a deeper engagement with problems to offer last solutions.

p. 67). Table 9.1 illustrates key principles that underpin each paradigm: instructional compared with learner-centred, with implications for leadership practice. Therefore, teaching and learning leaders who align with a learner-centred paradigm will lead with qualities such as 'sharing power, building community, and driving change through assessment and evaluation' (Harris & Cullen, 2010, p. 68). One or more of these qualities are deeply reflected in each of the case studies within this book.

Further insights into *leadership as change from an organisational perspective* are provided by Joan Gallos and Lee Bolman (2021), who examine the change process of initiatives that academic leaders want to implement. They argue that leaders need to structure the change process for their initiatives within the higher education context. They recommend 'three Ps of change for academic institutions: patience, persistence, and process' (Gallos & Bolman, 2021, p. 72) and as described below:

- *Patience:* The need to accommodate for time in any intended change that a teaching and learning leader may wish to implement, acknowledges that things move slowly within the higher education context, and thus the need for *patience*. Planning for appropriate timeframes for teaching and learning initiatives allows for leadership that ensures appropriate consultation and networking across the university.
- *Persistence:* is necessary to allow for multiple (re)introductions of the teaching and learning initiative and its ideas to reach to all stakeholders to 'capitalize on the fluid participation that characterizes shared governance structures . . . and the many autonomous campus players with diverse interests and unmet needs' and to work through the multiple issues, feelings and perspectives, particularly, for example, during early stages of leading change to build trust in the community (Gallos & Bolman, 2021, p. 73).
- *Process:* is significant because it concedes that change needs to be respectful of existing processes and the leader will need to navigate the change through these processes to ensure legitimacy. 'This is not to advocate bureaucracy, but a reminder that the norms of academic culture are strong. Transparency, dialogue, and attention to process go a long way' (Gallos & Bolman, 2021, p. 74).

In keeping the three Ps at front of mind, Gallos and Bolman (2021) commend that teaching and learning leaders can structure their academic change at three levels: structuring their own work as leaders; structuring relevant units within or across the higher education institution; and structuring the change process. Again, reflecting on the case studies in this book, you can see one or more levels of structuring the change process in each of the leadership narratives, showing how this strategy of structuring change may look like in teaching and learning leadership in higher education.

Leadership as relational

Another emerging theme across the case studies is *leadership as relational*. All chapter authors discuss teaching and learning leadership being about relations, be it with students, academic and professional staff, or executive leadership. Not surprisingly for teaching and learning leaders, students are at the heart of their advocacy and actions. Some chapter authors were also intuitive and realised they had to 'manage up' to the executive leadership to gain funds and allies in 'high places' to establish and sustain successful initiatives. Therefore, they used their understanding of institutional knowledge and processes to bring about change for improved learning and teaching (Gallos & Bolman, 2021; Smith, 2022). *Leadership as relational* reflects the complexity of teaching and learning leadership in higher education. Often, if they mentioned it at all, the chapter authors begrudgingly called themselves leaders in the telling of their stories. Rather, they talked of leading with and through the efforts of peers on initiatives collectively – and thus their leadership was often adaptive, responding to the feedback they received while experimenting with initiatives. This is not the typical quality of a traditional, hierarchical leader. Instead, it is more recognisable from the lens of complexity leadership theory where the 'notion of leadership is an emergent event, an outcome of relational interactions among agents. In this view, leadership is more than a skill, an exchange, or a symbol – leadership emerges through dynamic interactions' (Lichtenstein et al., 2006, p. 2).

Leadership as collaboration

Since the *leadership as relational* theme emerged across the case studies, it is of little surprise that *leadership as collaboration* is also a strongly represented theme across the case studies. The expression of collaboration in teaching and learning leadership is multi-faceted. At times the case studies demonstrate collaboration as building a community for learning from and with colleagues, peers or students to enhance learning and teaching practices. In other cases, the collaboration contributes to personal professional growth through, for example, seeking out mentors. At times, the case studies go further and discuss that collaboration may lead to *shared leadership* where power is shared or distributed to promote a culture and community of learning and sense-making to support teaching and learning innovation that is often transformational (Gallos & Bolman, 2021; Quinlan, 2020; Smith, 2022).

What do we need to foster teaching and learning leadership in higher education?

You can hear the passion for teaching and learning by each of the chapter authors in the case studies they shared in Part II of the book. Passion is widely held as an important quality of leaders because it motivates the direction of the leadership and clarifies their personal values to connect with organisational values to drive purpose and vision (Quinlan, 2020). It enables courage to take risks to introduce innovation because passion is 'a deep-rooted emotional investment that is rooted in love – for the work, the people who do it, the students who benefit, and the institution' (Gallos & Bolman, 2021, p. 295). Yet passion is an important quality for any leadership – so what else is a necessity for teaching and learning leadership that is also unique? The premise of this book is that there are limitations to our knowledge of teaching and learning leadership in higher education. The book and its case studies contribute to sharing lived experiences of teaching and learning leadership to provide significant insights into this emerging field in higher education leadership. In her research, Kathleen Quinlan (2020) raises that one of the three dimensions critical to leading for holistic learning in higher education is the expert knowledge of teaching and learning:

> [T]o create an environment for student learning, educational [i.e. teaching and learning] leaders need to understand something about learning and teaching and must work alongside other members of the team, especially those who are closest to students, reviewing data and evidence and learning and supporting teachers in implementing solutions that address performance gaps.
>
> (Quinlan, 2020, p. 79)

This is unique to teaching and learning leadership – and ensures passion that sustains inspirational and transformational leadership is built on strong fundamentals of expert working knowledge and practice to foster integrity and authenticity in teaching and learning leadership. Furthermore, what this book offers, is that teaching and learning leadership in higher education is not a linear trajectory. There are often many years spent in perfecting the art and science of teaching and learning while taking on teaching and learning leadership roles at micro (e.g. subject) or meso (e.g. programme or teaching team) levels to experiment with how teaching and learning leadership may reveal, in the practice of deep reflection and sense-making, in one's own personal, professional career in higher education. Perhaps, as teaching and learning leadership scholarship grows, it will continue to find new commonalities as well as highlight the uniqueness of the road travelled by each teaching and learning leader. Possibly, as the *Walker* in Antonio Machado's poem, there is no *one* particular road to teaching and learning leadership and self-reflection is critical to the journey. It is in the uniqueness of that path that we can discover the richness and beauty of teaching and learning leadership for holistic learning in and across higher education organisations and at the same time acknowledge that teaching and learning leadership is situated in, and shaped by, its context.

The impetus for higher education executive leadership, then, is to foster multi-faceted and diverse strategies to encourage professional learning and development across the organisation for teaching and learning leadership.

References

Gallos, J. V., & Bolman, L. G. (2021). *Reframing academic leadership* (2nd ed.). Jossey-Bass.

Harris, M., & Cullen, R. (2010). *Leading the learner-centered campus: An administrator's framework for improving student learning outcomes*. Jossey-Bass.

Lichtenstein, B. B., Uhl-Bien, M., Marion, R., Seers, A., Orton, J. D., & Schreiber, C. (2006). Complexity leadership theory: An interactive perspective on leading in complex adaptive systems. *Emergence: Complexity and Organization, 8*(4), 2–12.

Patton, W. (2021). The many faces of leadership: Leading people and change in Australian higher education. *Journal of Educational Administration and History, 53*(2), 121–131. doi:10.1080/00220620.2020.1793740

Quinlan, K. M. (2020). Leading for learning: Building on values and teaching expertise to effect change. In K. Jarrett & S. Newton (Eds.), *The practice of leadership in higher education: Real-world perspectives on becoming, being, and leaving* (pp. 71–86). Routledge.

Schön, D. A. (1983). *The reflective practitioner: How professionals think in action* (1st ed.). Reprinted in 1995 ed. Arena.

Smith, C. (2022). Noticing, curation, cultivation: Academic development leadership in the arts university. *Art, Design & Communication in Higher Education, 21*(1), 99–113. doi:10.1386/adch_00049_1

Index

academic development 4, 41, 46–47; curriculum and assessment 69; staff and professional 44, 63–64

building capability xii, 8, 66
building partnerships 36, 37

case studies: analysis 77–82; approach 5
casual teaching 8–9, 58–62
change management 36
collaboration 7–8, 15, 28–29, 55; approach 17–21, 35, 50, 52, 62–63; leadership xii, 9, 33–35, 56, 81; learning 26, 30; model 36; partnership 41, 45–47, 52, 54, 62; publications 34
competency(ies) 8–9, 66–69
complexity xii, 6, 8, 49, 60, 77, 78, 81
credibility 29, 68, 72
critical incidents 5–7, 9–10, 66–67, 73

deputy dean 8–9, 33–38
disability 42–45; special educational needs 42

evidence-informed practice 25, 27–29

formal leadership xii, 9, 28, 50, 66, 68
framework: capability 9, 67; cultural 64; higher education standards 37, 50; shared 44; teaching excellence 9; theoretical and conceptual 5, 7, 41, 50, 69

humanist 9, 46

inclusive assessment 8, 41, 44–46
institutional challenges and culture 43
international academic(s) 27, 58, 59, 61, 63–64
internationalisation 8, 24, 27–28, 30

leadership: academic xiii, 7, 9, 15–16, 49–51, 54–56, 67; alternative 41; distributed xii, 8, 35, 37, 56; inclusivity 24; informal xii, 58, 59, 68; invisible 42, 45–46; learning 5, 35, 78, 80, 8; practice 9, 34, 37, 80; pragmatic 18–21; quality 35, 81–83; quest 66–67, 72; relational 8, 56, 81; servant 18, 20–21; shared leadership 37, 45–46, 81; trajectory 41–42; transformative xi, 4
learning community 3, 50, 71
lived experience i, 5–7, 9–10, 46, 49, 54–56, 77–78, 82

Malaysia 9, 58, 60–61
mathematics and statistic support 8, 15–21
metrics 45

narrative 4, 6, 8, 41, 49

opportunities 15–16, 38–39, 43, 45–46, 51; and challenges 9; for interaction 18; for learning and development 21, 35–36, 70; life 33–34, 51, 56, 59, 77

Index

partnership 24, 27–29, 52
peer assisted learning 8, 24–27, 29–30

quality support: assurance 21, 50–51; of learning experience i, 9; professional 34; support 9; teaching 3, 69, 77, 79

scholarship of teaching and learning (SoTL) 17, 34, 78
sigma 15–21
student support services 41–42, 45
subject coordinator 58–62

transformative: education 21, 51; learning 8

For Product Safety Concerns and Information please contact our EU
representative GPSR@taylorandfrancis.com
Taylor & Francis Verlag GmbH, Kaufingerstraße 24, 80331 München, Germany

www.ingramcontent.com/pod-product-compliance
Lightning Source LLC
Chambersburg PA
CBHW071513150426
43191CB00009B/1517